By Sylvia Trygg Voudrie

DEDICATION

To the Amish ladies who made the original quilts which inspired this book,

To my precious granddaughters, Megan and Marissa, whom I hope to inspire one day to carry on the "new" family tradition of quilting,

To my wonderful husband, who is ever so supportive of my love of quilting,

To the Lord for His faithfulness and goodness to me.

Chitra Publications
2 Public Avenue
Montrose, Pennsylvania 18801

First printing: 1994
Library of Congress Cataloging-in-Publication Data

Voudrie, Sylvia Trygg, date.
Tiny Amish traditions / by Sylvia Trygg Voudrie.
p. cm.
Includes bibliographical references.
ISBN 0-9622565-8-7 : $9.95
1. Quilting--Patterns. 2. Patchwork--Patterns. 3. Miniature quilts. 4. Quilts, Amish. I. Title
TT835.V67 1994
746' .46' 0228--dc20 94-29993
CIP

Editor: Janice P. Johnson
Design and Illustration: Diane M. Albeck
Photographs: Stephen J. Appel Photography, Vestal, New York

TABLE OF CONTENTS

INTRODUCTION

It would be a wonderful thing if all quilters could own at least one of the beautiful antique Amish quilts that were lovingly and painstakingly created by Amish ladies between the late 1800s and 1940. Most of them are in private collections. Some have found their way into museums, where we can study them and appreciate their unique beauty.

What is it about these quilts that reaches out to us? Perhaps it is the vibrancy of the bold, solid colors. It could be the tiny, precise quilting stitches that lavishly adorn these quilts. Maybe part of the enchantment is that these outwardly unadorned women would create such lovely works of art. With all the many household and farm chores, the responsibilities of rearing large families, the caring for the elderly in the family, these ladies still found time to quietly express themselves in a creative way. They did not need our modern-day quilt stores with all the latest fabrics and gadgets to inspire them. They simply cut up their old cotton and wool clothing and recycled them into masterpieces.

Having visited Amish communities in three different states, I also admire these Amish ladies of yesterday and today for their faithfulness to God, to their families, and to their communities. They may be unadorned outwardly, but they are certainly adorned inwardly.

This book of patterns is intended to help us appreciate those original quilts and their makers. Each pattern is a simulation of an original quilt that has been photographed. I have noted at the beginning of each pattern where and when the original was made, and the present-day owner. This information has come from quilt books containing their photographs. You will find these books listed in the bibliography.

I have scaled each large quilt down to a miniature pattern. Some patterns contain the same number of pieces that are in the antique quilt; some patterns contain fewer blocks or pieces to allow them to be made in miniature. My quilts are not exact replicas. I have tried to color match the fabrics to the quilt pieces in the photographs. This cannot be totally accurate due to variations in photography and printing. Finding the exact shade of a fabric color was not always possible, either. The backing colors may not be the same, as I have never seen the actual antique quilts. Lastly, the quilting designs on my tiny quilts are not the same as those on the large quilts.

May you enjoy making these *Tiny Amish Traditions* as much as I have and also enjoy having them in your own "private" collection.

Sylvia

Rotary Cutter

A large size rotary cutter makes it possible to cut strips and pieces accurately and quickly. Do not tighten the screw on a cutter too tightly or you will have difficulty cutting fabric. The screw should be just tight enough for the blade to turn firmly but easily. Always keep a spare blade on hand to replace a dull one. We quilters tend to be very miserly about changing blades. I am always surprised at how well a new blade cuts; it will save much cutting time and frustration. A pocket eyeglass case makes a great holder for your cutter.

Cutting Mats

The most versatile size is probably 18" x 24". Even for miniature quilts, you still need a mat large enough to make long strip or bias cuts. A very small one is handy to move around for small cuts and is great for the last step in joining the binding on a quilt. A 12" x 18" is handy to take to classes.

Rulers for Rotary Cutting

Accurate rulers are essential for the precision cuts that result in accurately made miniature quilts. The following sizes are excellent:

6" x 12" for most strip cuts

3" x 18" for long first cuts and long bias cuts

4" square: This little gem made by Omnigrid® has 1/16" side markings, which are needed for many of these quilts.

6" square with 45° angle line marked on the diagonal for cutting half-square triangle units. The 4" square can also be used for this purpose.

Sandpaper

This is one of my favorite tools. You just can't beat using a fine-grained sandpaper with adhesive backing on the bottom of all your rulers to keep them from slipping during use. Miniature pieces require slip-proof cutting. A package of fine-grain sandpaper with adhesive backing can be purchased at a hardware store very inexpensively. It is made for electric sanders.

Cut sandpaper into small squares or use a standard size hole puncher to punch uniform circles. Position them on the bottom of your rulers along the cutting edges, about every two inches. Place a few pieces on each side of the diagonal or bias line of your square ruler to help keep the bias line securely centered on the seamline when you are cutting half-square triangle units.

Chart Tape

This is a very thin, colored tape that is used for making graph charts. I use this to mark a ruler for making special cuts. A 1/16"-wide colored tape makes a fine line, which is easy to follow. It adheres well but removes easily when no longer needed. Purchase this at an office supply store.

Drafting Tape

When you cannot get an accurate 1/4" seam with a presser foot on your sewing machine, use drafting tape as a seam guide. It leaves no residue. This can be purchased at an office supply store.

Sewing Machine

You do not need a fancy machine, but it must be in good condition to produce good work. Be sure that the tension is correctly adjusted and that your machine sews a good seam. If not, have it serviced.

Straight-stitch Throat Plate

This is not essential to have for your sewing machine, but having one will produce straighter seams and stitches. Check the machine's accessory box or obtain one from a dealer.

Sewing Machine Needles

A "fine" needle will prevent distortion of small pieces of fabric; size 70/10 or 80/12 will not leave holes in the fabric. Change needles with every quilt.

Thread

I once heard a quilter say, "Thread is thread." Not so! Buy good quality thread. My favorite for miniatures is Mettler cotton embroidery thread, which is 60 weight/2-ply. A fine thread reduces bulk in the seams. Save money by using cones of good quality thread and a cone holder. White, off-white or light gray thread are good neutrals and can be bought economically.

Seam Ripper

This is not only for ripping out bad seams and mistakes. It also makes a great tool for guiding "frisky" fabric pieces under the presser foot.

Thread Clippers

Using thread clippers to snip chain-pieced units apart is much quicker than using scissors.

Long, Fine Straight Pins

The pins that are labeled "quilter's pins" are long, but they are too heavy for tiny pieces. Look for long, fine silk pins or fine pins with glass heads.

Magnetized Pin Holder

This is not essential, but it is absolutely terrific! You can practically throw your pins at it. Stainless steel pins will not work.

Ironing Surface and Steam Iron

Some quilters do not use steam, but I find it necessary for setting seams and straightening any distortions. Keep the iron on the lowest heat setting for steam; you do not want to give your cotton fabrics a "shiner." An alternative is using a spray bottle filled with distilled water.

Spot Remover

Keep a good spot remover on hand, one that does not leave any residue on fabric. You never know when a spot might appear on one of your tiny treasures! Your own saliva works well on a blood spot from your pricked finger.

Glue Stick

This is an invaluable aid when matching difficult seams. Place a dab on one seam allowance and position the adjoining seam allowance in the correct position.

Marking Pencils

Mechanical pencils with 0.5 mm lead make fine lines on light fabric. A Berol® Verithin® Silver #753 works well on dark fabric.

FABRICS

Choose only light to medium weight, closely woven 100 percent cotton fabrics. Blends do not look or feel as good, or take stitching as well as cotton. Batting also tends to "beard" through blends; the fibers migrate to the surface of the quilt, making it fuzzy.

Because these patterns are for Amish quilts, you will be using only solid colors in these miniatures. I have tried to simulate the colors from a photograph of each antique Amish quilt as closely as possible. This, of course, cannot always be accurate due to variations in photography and printing, nor could I always find the exact shade I wanted. If you wish to use the same colors, they are listed in the Fabric Requirements for each pattern. These patterns could also be used to make non-Amish quilts by choosing patterned fabrics.

Keep in mind that good contrast is essential between two fabrics that are next to each other. Otherwise, they will blend together and you will not see the individual tiny pieces of the quilt. You do want your hard work to show. One of the wonderful things about making these Amish miniatures in solid colors is that each separate piece in a quilt is clearly seen.

Since I have seen the original antique quilts in photographs only, I chose a backing color for each quilt that I thought was complementary to the quilt top. It is the same fabric as the last border on the quilt. This will allow you to use the same color thread for quilting. The backing color is suggested for each pattern.

To Wash or Not To Wash

Most quilters say to wash all your fabric before using it, without exception, or you may be sorry when you wash the quilt later. Certain dyes may bleed onto other fabrics.

My preference is to use unwashed fabric in miniature quilts. It has more body and is easier to handle. These quilts will not be handled roughly, so vigorous washing will not be needed.

If you choose not to wash your fabrics, it is a good idea to color test them before use. Cut 2" squares of each fabric and drop them into separate glasses of hot water. Allow them to soak for about 15 minutes. If color bleeds into the water from any of the fabrics, either do not use it or wash all fabrics in warm water with a mild soap. I prefer Orvus Paste for washing quilt fabrics. It can be purchased in small quantities at quilt stores or in an economical gallon size at a farm supply store. Rinse thoroughly and tumble in the dryer until almost dry. Spray the cloth with a fabric sizing as you press or use a spray bottle filled with 1/4 cup of liquid starch diluted with one cup of distilled water. (These sprays are also great for pressing the center crease out of fabric.)

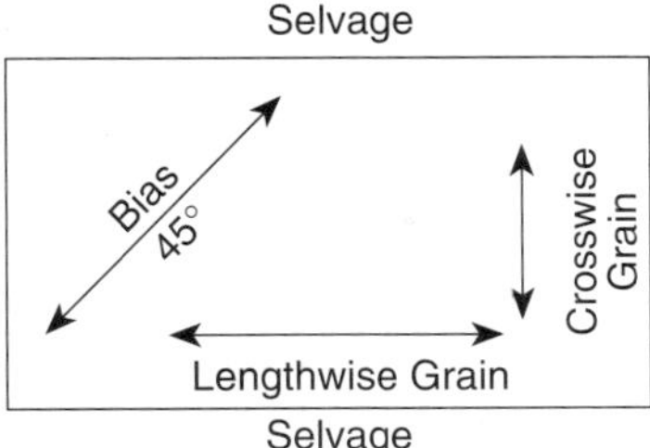

Fig. 1

Working With Grainlines

Fabric is made from threads that are woven together lengthwise and crosswise. The lengthwise grain runs parallel to the selvages of the fabric; the crosswise grain runs from selvage to selvage. The lengthwise grain is the most stable, having almost no stretch to it. The crosswise grain has some stretch to it. The third type of grain is called the bias. It runs at a 45° angle to the lengthwise and crosswise grains. This bias grain is very "stretchy" (Fig. 1).

Grainline is important in the cutting of fabric strips and pieces. Straight strips, squares and rectangles are cut on the lengthwise or crosswise grain of fabric. Because triangles have three sides, it follows that one side will always fall on the bias or "stretchy" grain if the other two sides are cut on the straight grain. Half-square triangles should have the short sides on the straight grain, while quarter-square triangles should have the short sides on the bias grain. The reason for this is to keep the straight grain on the outside of the unit, where it needs stability (Fig. 2 and Fig. 3).

This principle also applies to setting triangles and corner triangles that form the outside edges of a quilt (See Setting the Quilt on pg. 16).

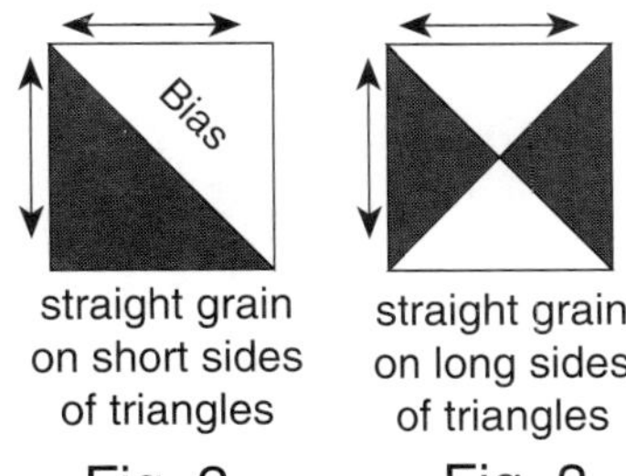

Fig. 2 Fig. 3

Cutting Straight Strips

Most of the pieces used to make the quilts in this book are cut from strips, so you must know how to cut perfectly straight narrow strips across the width of the fabric (usually 44"). The lengthwise and crosswise grain on most fabric is not perfectly straight. Usually, this does not pose a problem unless it is very obviously distorted. Sometimes there are portions of the distorted fabric where the grainlines are more true. If so, try to cut your strips from these sections. You can always cut individual pieces in the distorted areas.

My instructions are for right-handed quilters. Simply reverse the procedure if you are left-handed.

1. Fold the fabric in half, lining up the selvages. The center fold is sometimes distorted when fabric is wrapped onto the bolt, so do not go by that fold to line up the selvages. You may have to move the selvage of the top layer to the left or right and make a new center fold.
2. Always start with a perfectly straight-cut left edge. Take your square ruler and line it up with the fold on the bottom, near the left edge of the fabric. With your left hand, place the long ruler against the square ruler. Remove the square ruler with your right hand. Take the rotary cutter and begin cutting just below the bottom fold and continue along the edge of the long ruler, cutting away from yourself. Apply pressure with your left hand to keep the ruler in place. (Those little pieces of sandpaper are also doing their job at keeping the ruler from slipping.) Walk your fingers up the ruler, parallel to the rotary cutter in your right hand, and make the first cut. This is the longest, most difficult cut to make (Fig. 4 and Fig. 5).
3. Now bring the bottom fold up to meet the selvages and line up the four cut edges. From now on, you can make shorter cuts through all the layers. Find the line on the ruler for the width of strip needed,

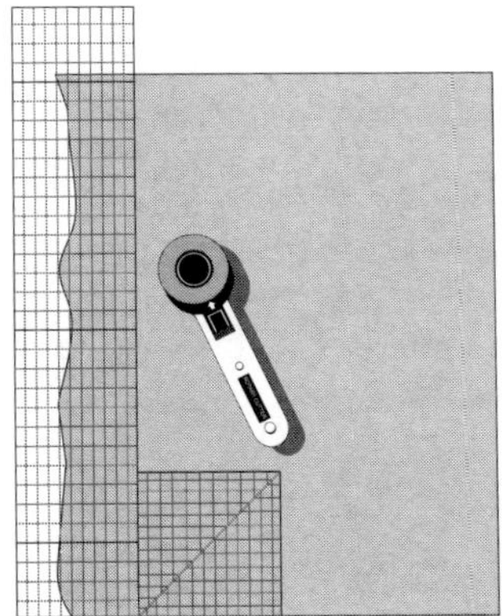
Fig. 4

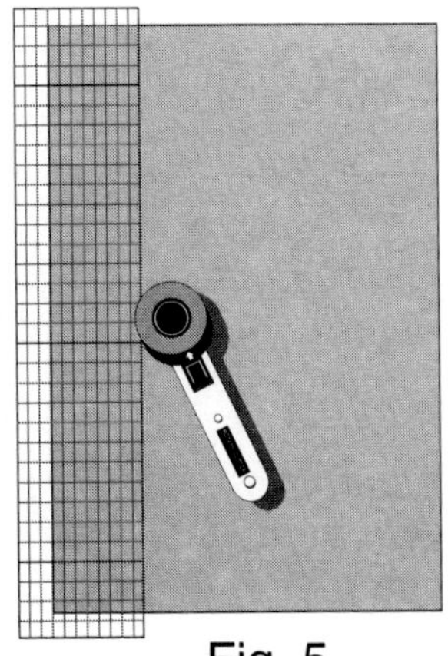
Fig. 5

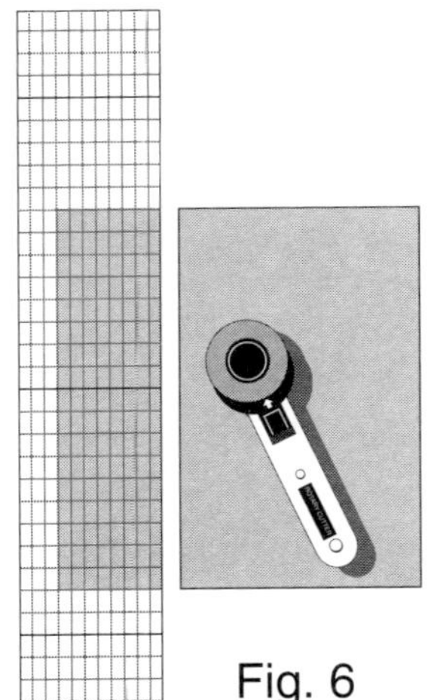
Fig. 6

align the ruler with the fabric's straight-cut left edge and make your cut. If you are cutting many strips, check the left edge frequently and re-straighten if needed (Fig. 6).

Cutting Bias Strips

Bias strips are cut at a 45° angle to the grainline. Align the 45° angle line of a long ruler along a selvage of the fabric and make a cut. Measure the width of the strip needed (finished size plus seam allowances) from the 45° angle cut. Cut along the edge of the ruler (Fig. 7 and Fig. 8).

Cutting Squares and Rectangles

When a pattern requires a large number of squares and rectangles, they are subcut from strips. The width of the strip is determined by the finished width of the squares or rectangles needed, plus their seam allowance.

FORMULA: Strip width to cut = Finished size of squares or rectangles plus 1/2" for seam allowance.

Use the square ruler to subcut squares or rectangles of the required length. If you do not need many pieces, they can be cut individually rather than from strips. Just remember to add 1/2" for seam allowances before cutting.

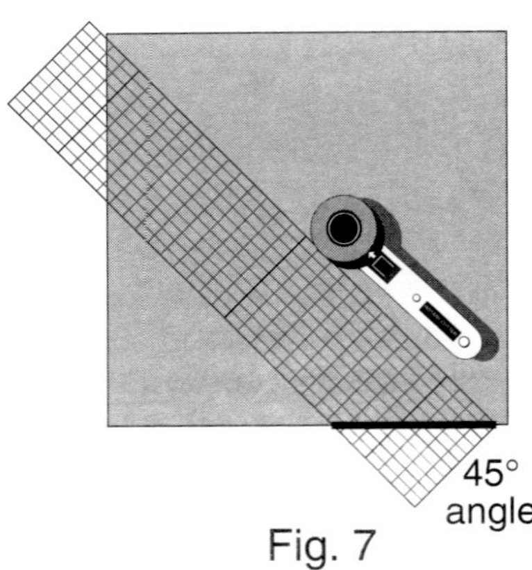

Fig. 7

Cutting Strips That Have Been Sewn Together

Many of the patterns in this book are subcut from strip set-ups that have been sewn together first. It is necessary not only to cut precise strips, but also to sew these strips together with precise 1/4" seam allowances. Sew slowly and accurately. Any discrepancy is magnified when stitching miniature quilts. Remember the admonition to keep on the straight and narrow!

The Four Patch and Nine Patch are two examples of blocks made by first sewing strips together into set-ups, subcutting them into segments and then arranging and sewing these segments together to form the blocks. For the Four Patch, sew together two contrasting strips of equal widths. Press the seam allowance toward the darker fabric. Subcut this set-up into two segments which are equal to the finished size of a single square plus its seam allowance.

EXAMPLE: If the finished size of a single square is 1/2", you would need two segments that are each cut 1" (Fig. 9).

Place the two segments right sides together, with contrasting squares opposing each other. The pressed seam allowances will butt

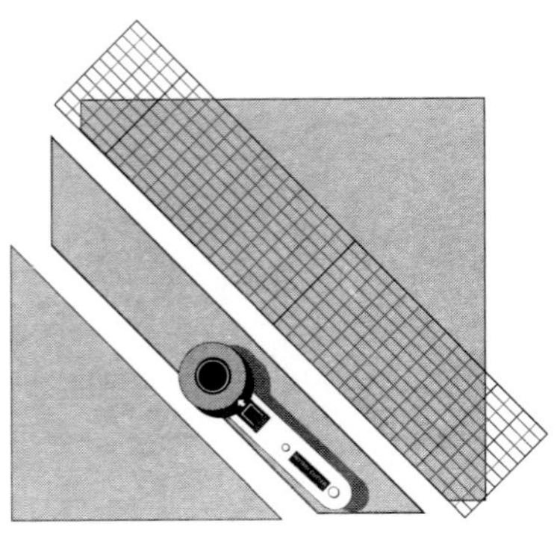
Fig. 8

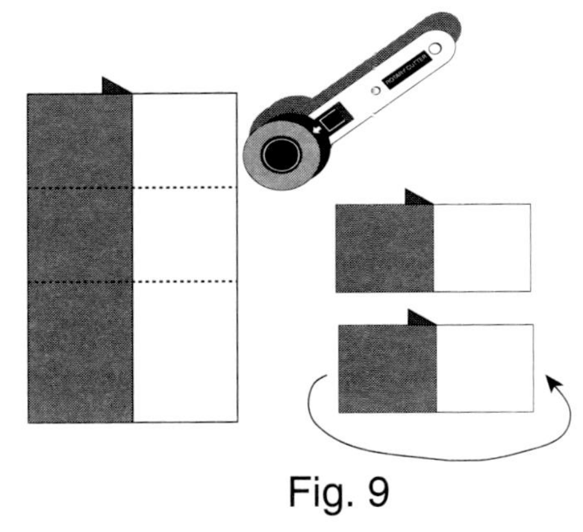
Fig. 9

Fig. 10

each other in opposite directions. Sew the seam and press (Fig. 10).

For the Nine Patch, two set-ups are required; one for Rows 1 and 3 and one for Row 2 (Fig. 11). Cut two segments from one set-up and one segment from the other. The technique is the same as that for the Four Patch.

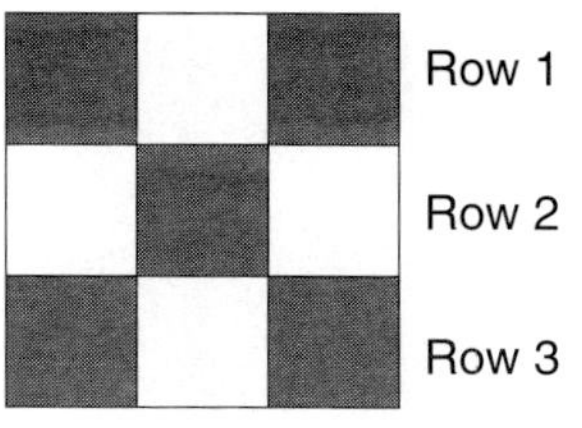

Fig. 11

Cutting Half-Square Triangle Units

The method I have used for this Amish collection is an adaptation of that devised by quilter Nancy J. Martin of That Patchwork Place, Inc. Her technique uses her 6" Bias Square™ ruler. Other square rulers will also do the job if they have a center diagonal line and 1/8" markings. If you have the Bias Square ruler, be sure that you measure to the outside of the lines and not to the inside.

Nancy's method is to cut bias strips of two-fabric combinations and sew them together lengthwise on the long bias edge. Rather than cutting bias strips, I subcut squares from strips that are approximately 1 1/4" wider than the size of the finished half-square triangle units that are needed.

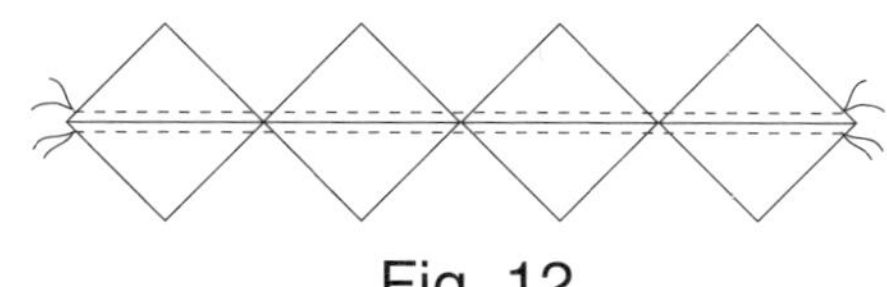

Fig. 12

1. For each two half-square triangle units needed; cut a square of each fabric in a combination that is 1 1/4" larger than the size of the finished units that are needed.
2. Using a fine-line pencil, draw a diagonal line on the wrong side of the lighter square.
3. Place the marked light square face down on the dark square and sew a 1/4" seam on one side of the marked diagonal line. HINT: Sewing these seams with a 1/8" seam will eliminate having to trim them back. Continue chain-piecing the seams of the other units. Chain-piece 1/4" or 1/8" seams on the other side of the diagonal lines of all the units. Clip units apart (Fig. 12).
4. Cut each unit in half on its diagonal line. Press seams toward the dark fabric. Trim each half-square triangle unit to the cut size needed (finished size plus 1/2") with a square ruler. Lay the diagonal line of the square ruler on the bias seam of the square and cut the top two edges. Turn the unit and align the cut edges with the size square needed. Make the last two cuts (Fig. 13). Trim seams to 1/8" if 1/4" seams were used.

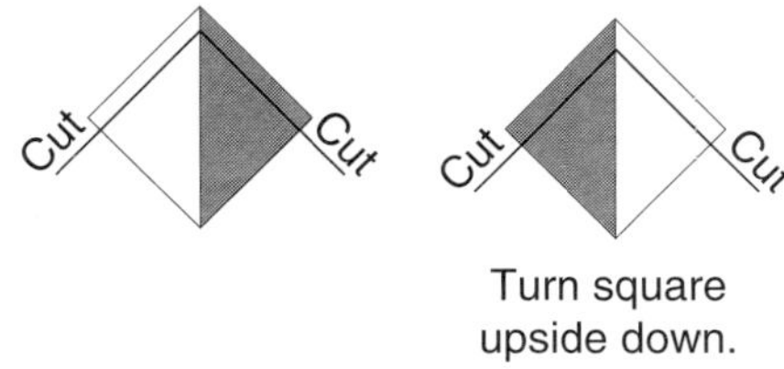

Fig. 13

NOTE: There are other methods for making these half-square triangle units. I am not describing them in this book. You may use any method you prefer to achieve the same result.

Using Connector Squares

Mary Ellen Hopkins defines this technique as using connector corners. These little squares really are quick and accurate. The technique is high on my list of technique "musts!" It is used in several of the patterns in this book. There is very little waste of fabric because we are dealing with small pieces.

To alternate a Four Patch or Nine Patch block with a Snowball block (Fig. 14):

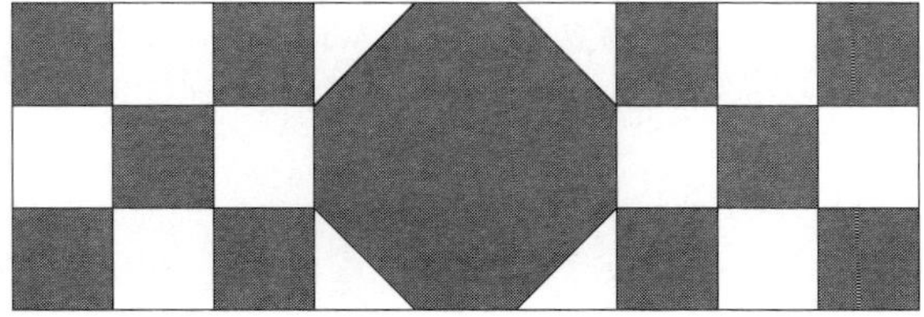

Fig. 14

Fig. 15

1. Cut a large square the same size as the Four Patch or Nine Patch block, plus 1/2" seam allowance. Then cut four little squares the size of one of the Four Patch or Nine Patch squares, plus 1/2" seam allowances (Fig. 15).

2. Place each little square in a corner of the large square, right sides together, and sew diagonal seams (Fig. 16). There are three options for sewing these diagonal seams:

a. Eyeball the seamline.

b. First draw a diagonal guideline.

c. Finger press a diagonal crease.

Press each square back to its corner. For our tiny quilts, trim the two lower layers (the seam allowance) to 1/8".

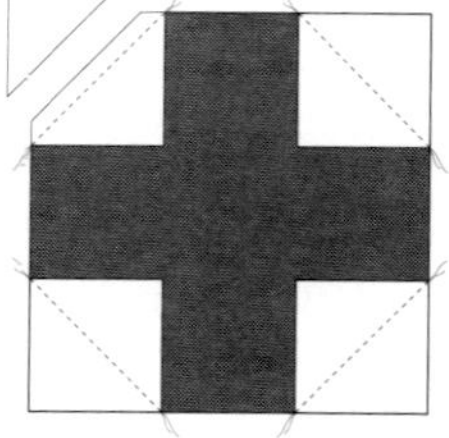

Fig. 16

To make Flying Geese Units (Fig. 17):

1. Cut a rectangle the finished size required, plus 1/2" seam allowances.

2. Cut two squares one-half the length of the finished unit, plus 1/2" seam allowances.

3. Stitch one square in place, press it back to its corner and trim two lower layers (the seam allowance) to 1/8".

4. Sew the other square on the other side the same way; the seams will "cross" at the seam allowance, making a perfect point. Press and trim as before (Fig. 18).

Cutting Many Same-Size Pieces

An easy way to cut many same-size pieces accurately and quickly is to tape 1/16" wide chart tape strips to the bottom of your cutting ruler precisely where you will line up the ruler to make the cuts. This way you will not have to measure each time you make a cut. It is also great for marking your ruler to cut unusual shapes.

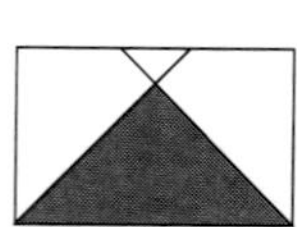

Fig. 17

Sew

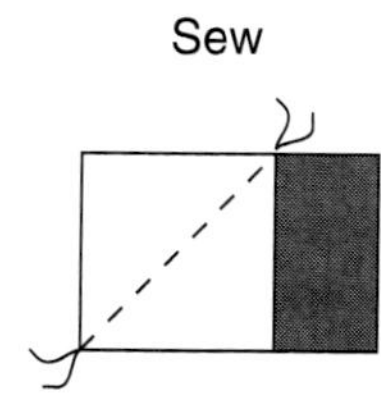

Press

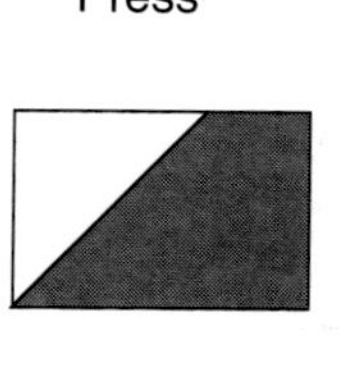

Trim

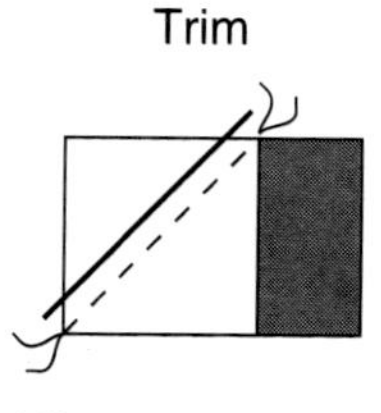

Repeat

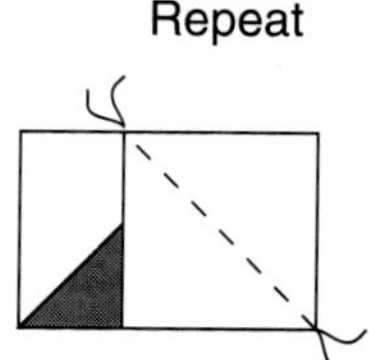

Fig. 18

Seam Allowance

The patterns in my first book, *Tiny Traditions*, were to be sewn with a 1/8" seam allowance. After teaching these patterns to many quilters, I found that many are more comfortable using the standard 1/4" seam allowance. Some sewing machines want to fight the little 1/8" seam. Therefore, the patterns in this book are written for a 1/4" seam allowance. The 1/4" seams will have to be trimmed back to 1/8" in certain areas to eliminate bulky seams, which are unattractive and difficult to quilt through.

An accurate 1/4" seam is a must for miniatures. When making large quilts with larger blocks and pieces, there is room for fudging a little when one piece is a bit too large or too small. We fudge by easing the larger piece to fit the smaller one or stretching the smaller piece to fit the larger one. Well, in miniatures there is no room for fudging—playing with only 1/4" to 3/4" finished pieces is quite different from playing with 2" pieces. Just try stretching or easing in only 1/2" of space.

Here are some suggestions for achieving a perfect 1/4" seam. First experiment with your machine's presser feet. The right edge on one of them may be exactly 1/4" from the needle. If your machine has different needle positions, one combined with the right presser foot may be perfect. There is always the possibility of finding a 1/4" presser foot made for another make of sewing machine that will fit your machine. The sewing machine companies are beginning to cater more to quilters' needs. Several now offer a quilter's presser foot for their machine. An alternative is to purchase the Little Foot, a 1/4" presser foot designed to fit a variety of machines, which can be purchased at a quilt store or through mail order.

An accurate and inexpensive guide is drafting tape placed on your machine 1/4" away from the needle. The strip must be placed just in front of the presser foot area on most machines because presser feet on newer machines are wider than 1/4". This tape guide is helpful even if a presser foot alone can give you an accurate 1/4" seam.

Test your tape guide by cutting three 1" x 6" fabric strips. Sew the long sides together, using the tape as your guide. Press the 1/4" seam allowances to one side. Measure the width of the strip set. It should measure exactly 2" wide. If it is a bit narrower, relocate the tape a little closer to the needle. If it is slightly wider, relocate the tape a little farther from the needle. Keep in mind that the seam allowance must include the width of the seamline itself. When the guide is precisely located, you can build up several layers of tape to form a ridge, or use a single narrow strip of Moleskin (a product for the feet). This ridge will keep fabric straight as you sew.

Throat Plate

Years ago sewing machines had throat plates only for straight stitching. Then came the advent of zigzag sewing machines. The throat plate on zigzag machines had to accommodate the width of the stitches. Most of these machines came with both throat plates. Now the new machines sew up to 9 mm in width and come with only a zigzag plate. If you can obtain a straight-stitch throat plate for your machine, it is wonderful for machine piecing and quilting. The fabric does not get pushed into the hole of the throat plate. It gives you straighter stitches and seams.

Stitch Length

You will be using chain-piecing methods whenever possible, which means the seams will not be secured with a backstitch. Therefore, a short stitch length is necessary. I work at 14 stitches per inch. Do not go any shorter; the seams would be difficult to take out in case of error. These seams will be crossed by other seams, which will secure them.

Sew Slowly

Slow, controlled sewing is necessary to ensure perfect seams. If your sewing machine has a slow speed setting, use that feature. If not, slow yourself down and become accustomed to it. I have seen quilters press their foot to the floor in an effort to get the most done. This usually does not produce the best work. Every discrepancy in stitching makes a difference in miniatures.

Butting Seams

In order to match seams when joining one unit to another, press the seam allowances in opposite directions, toward the darker fabric whenever possible. This will cause the seam allowances to butt each other at the seamline. This makes it easy to match the seams, and it also distributes the bulk of the seam allowances. Occasionally, pressing a seam toward the darker fabric will not butt the seams; that seam should be pressed toward the light fabric.

Intersecting Seams

The usual way to match intersections of more than two seams is to pin through the point of the top fabric and through the point of the bottom fabric on a positioning pin. Line up the points so they are straight on the pin and place pins on both sides of positioning pin. Remove the positioning pin and stitch exactly through the intersection.

An easier method is to use a dab of glue stick on one seam allowance and position the joining seam allowance in the exact position.

Chain-Piecing

Think of mass production methods in garment factories. One person sews the same unit on many garments, assembly line fashion. The same principle can be applied to quiltmaking. Piece the like units of the different blocks in assembly line fashion to save time and thread. Sometimes one individual block has so many like pieces, you can piece them by this method, too.

Sew like units together in a chain by feeding pairs of units under the presser foot. Sew the first seam, add another pair, sew that seam, etc. Because of the size of our pieces, it is best to raise the presser foot each time and very carefully position pairs to achieve the accuracy you need for your seams. Clip units apart after you have completed the chain (Fig. 19).

Do not worry about the seams coming apart. Remember you are using 14 stitches to the inch. Soon you will be crossing each of these seams with another seam, which will secure them.

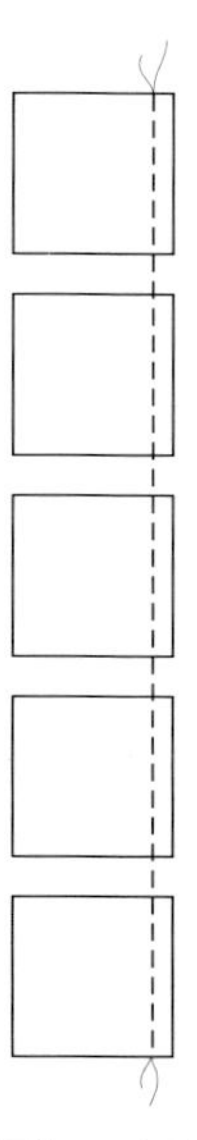
Fig. 19

Pressing

Careful pressing of seams is extremely important in making miniature quilts. The seams must take up the correct amount of space to make tiny pieces fit together like a puzzle. The words "press" and "iron" are not synonymous. Pressing quilt seams requires a light touch, not a back and forth motion. Quilters differ on the use of steam. I prefer to use steam. If used properly, it can set seams and straighten distortions.

Press each seam in the closed position before pressing it to one side. Turn the piece over on the right side and finger press the seam to the correct side. The heat from the first pressing will make this very easy to do. Then press again with the iron. This way there are never any creases at the seams.

When pressing the seams of long strips, lay the seam perpendicular to your body, pressing vertically over the ironing surface. This usually eliminates the possibility of pressing an arc into the strips.

SETTING THE QUILT

Fig. 20

The visual arrangement of the blocks in a quilt top is called the "set." The basic sets are straight and diagonal (Fig. 20 and Fig. 21).

It is easy to figure the dimensions of a straight set quilt by simply multiplying the size of the block times the number of blocks in the width and in the length. If you have added sashing between the blocks, these widths will have to be added.

Diagonal sets, where the blocks are set on point, take some calculation. You need to know the diagonal width of a finished block to do this.

FORMULA: Finished block size x 1.414 = diagonal width.

EXAMPLE: 3" finished block x 1.414 = 4.242 or 4 1/4"

Now it is simple to multiply the number of blocks times the diagonal width to find the dimensions of a diagonally set quilt.

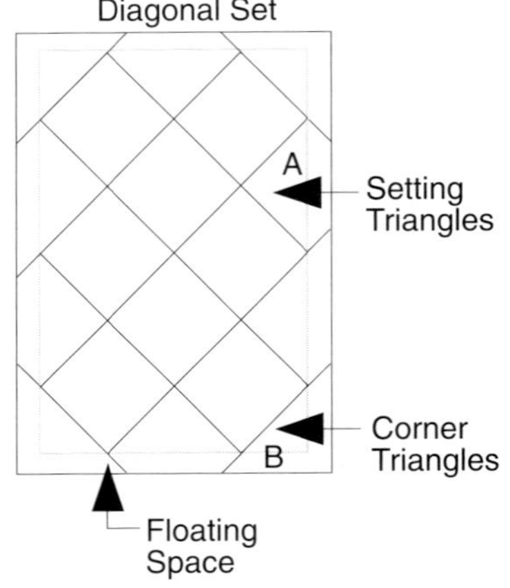

Fig. 21

Setting Triangles

Setting triangles are cut from a square. To determine the size of the square, add 1 1/4" to the diagonal width of the block. Using the diagonal width from the above example, you would add 1 1/4" to the 4 1/4", resulting in a 5 1/2" square. One square is cut diagonally both ways to make (4) setting triangles (Fig. 22).

Determine the setting triangles needed and cut the appropriate number of squares. By cutting the squares diagonally both ways, the straight grain of the fabric will be on the long edges of the triangles. These long edges will be on the outside perimeter of your quilt, which helps keep the quilt from stretching.

The above triangles are the exact size needed for the outside point of 3" square finished blocks to meet the border. If you prefer to "float" the blocks, making them appear to lay on top of the background rather than meet the border, cut the squares 1 3/4" to 2" larger than the diagonal width of the finished block.

Even up the sides of the pieced quilt top with a long ruler and rotary cutter. Be sure to leave a 1/4" seam allowance all around the quilt top.

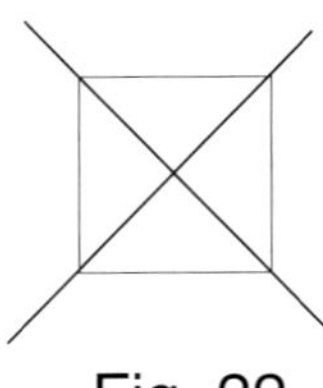

Fig. 22

Corner Triangles

Corner triangles are also cut from squares. To determine the size squares required for cutting the triangles, add 1" to the finished block size.

FORMULA: Finished block size plus 1" = the size squares to cut for making corner triangles.

For a 3" finished block you would cut (2) 4" squares in half diagonally to make the (4) corner triangles (Fig. 23).

By cutting these squares diagonally in half only one way, the straight grain of the fabric will be on the two short edges of each triangle. The long bias edges will be stitched to your quilt at each corner and the straight grain will again be on the outside of the quilt.

To sew these corner triangles to the quilt top, first finger press a crease in the center of each triangle on the long bias edge. Also finger press a crease in the center of each block that will be stitched to a corner triangle. Match the creases and pin. Pin the two edges where a block meets a triangle, leaving an equal amount of triangle exposed on both sides. Stitch the seam and press it toward the outside of the quilt. Repeat for each corner. Using the square ruler, trim the corners even with the sides of the quilt.

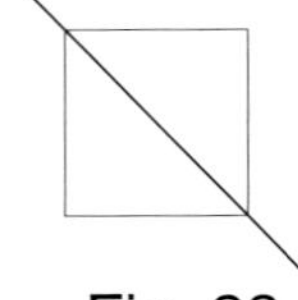

Fig. 23

For this Amish collection of miniature quilts, I have tried to keep the borders of each quilt in the same proportion as those of the large antique quilts they simulate. If you choose to vary the look of the quilt or to make it in non-Amish fabrics, you can change the border widths given in the pattern. I have also added the borders to each quilt in the same method that they were added to the original.

Straight-Cut Corner Method

The easiest way to add borders is by the straight-cut corner method (Fig. 24).

First, measure the length of the quilt top through the center. Cut (2) border strips that measurement, and sew to each side of the quilt. Press seams toward the border strips. Now measure the width of the quilt with its side borders, again through the center. Cut (2) border strips that measurement, and sew to the top and bottom of the quilt. Additional borders of varying widths can be added in similar fashion.

Fig. 24

Mitered-Corner Method

Another way to add borders to a quilt is by mitering the corners. The corners of the borders are stitched together at a 45° angle (Fig. 25). The easiest method I have found for adding mitered borders to a quilt is illustrated below.

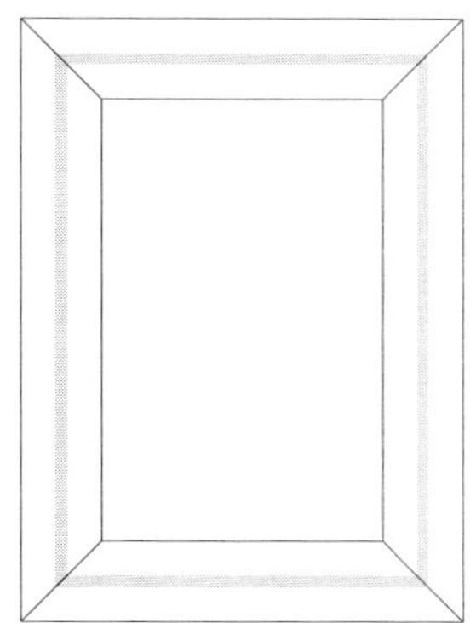

Fig. 25

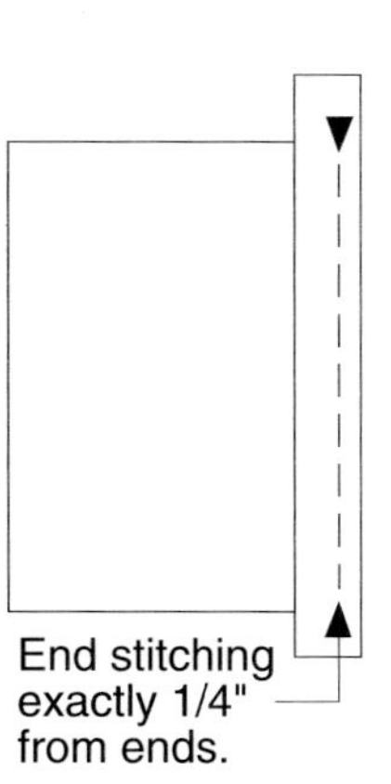

Fig. 26

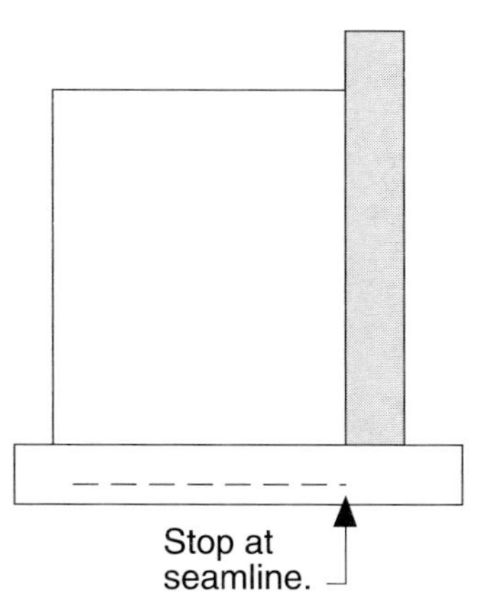

Fig. 27

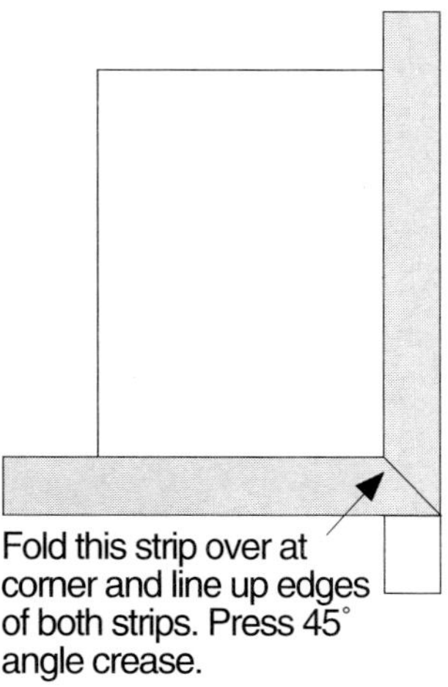

Fig. 28

FINISHING

Selecting Batting

Only very thin batting should be used in a miniature quilt, so it will fold and drape easily rather than be rigid. There are several low-loft batts that can be used. Some regular-loft batts can be peeled into two layers, which makes them suitable for tiny quilts.

My preference is Thermore®, which is an ultra-thin polyester batting by Hobbs. This batting is non-bearding and is super easy to quilt through.

If you wish to give your quilt a puckered look after it is washed, try Hobbs Heirloom Cotton. This batting is a little heavier than Thermore, so I would recommend it only for larger miniatures.

Backing Fabric

For each quilt in this book, I have suggested a backing color that I feel is complementary to the quilt top. Usually, the backing and borders match.

Because the quilting stitches sometimes cause the backing to draw up to a smaller size, cut your backing 1" to 1 1/2" larger than the quilt top on all sides. The excess will be trimmed after the binding is attached to the quilt top.

Basting

The easiest way to baste the layers of a miniature quilt together is to "pin baste." I use 1", rustproof safety pins. There are larger pins on the market, called quilter's safety pins, but they make holes in the fabric. You do not need large safety pins because you are using thin batting and there is less bulk than with a large quilt. Do not use straight pins for basting. They will either get caught, come out or stab you!

Secure the quilt layers with safety pins in areas where you will not be quilting. (You can always remove a pin if it is in the way.) Remember to keep the quilt straight, both horizontally and vertically, and to keep it pucker-free as you pin it.

Marking Quilt Lines

These tiny Amish quilts require much more quilting than other miniatures. Usually, I think less is best with most miniature quilts. However, one of the wonderful features of Amish quilts is the beautiful hand quilting.

My suggestion is to first quilt these Amish miniatures in the ditch or near the seams, which outlines the piecing in the quilt. This does not require marking. In addition, the open areas and borders should be embellished with quilted designs. There are border stencils and block stencils now available in miniature size that can be used for marking. You may also trace around designs cut from template plastic. Another option is to cut small shapes from Contact® paper, remove the backing and stick the shape where you want it. Then quilt around it and relocate it to other areas.

It is easiest to mark the quilt top before you layer it. Mark very lightly with a 0.5 mm mechanical pencil on light fabrics. I use Pentel Hi Polymer lead. The empty lead containers make great needle cases. On dark fabrics I use a Berol Verithin Silver #753 pencil. You must keep the point sharp to produce a fine line.

When marking the quilting design on borders, remember to leave a 1/4" seam allowance free for adding the binding.

To Hoop or Not to Hoop

If you are accustomed to quilting on a hoop, you will probably want to use one for miniatures, as well. The problem is, what size? Some quilts are too small for most hoops, and flimsy hoops designed for needlework will not hold a quilt very well.

My solution is to use a scroll-type needlework frame. The edges of the quilt top and backing are pinned to fabric strips that are fastened to the frame. Q-Snap™ frames also work quite well. They are now available in an 8" square set, which can be combined with an 11" or 17" set to give you an 8" x 11" or and 8" x 17" frame. It is not necessary to fasten the sides of the quilt on either of these frames. The tension is controlled by turning the lengthwise rods. The principle is the same as a large floor frame.

The other alternative is not to use a hoop at all, which is my preference. My left hand pushes those little stitches onto the quilting needle in my right hand. They make a great team!

Hand Quilting or Machine Quilting

Personal preference is the biggest factor. I machine quilt many of my larger quilts, but I enjoy hand quilting miniatures. In some of my quilt lectures I have said that it can take as much time to piece a miniature quilt as a bed-size quilt, but it takes very little time to hand quilt it.

For hand quilting I prefer to use 100% cotton thread. If I cannot find the right color quilting thread for a miniature, I will use a size 50 weight/3-ply style cotton to match the quilt. The quilting thread used for miniatures does not have to be as strong as that used for larger quilts.

For machine quilting, use a fine nylon thread on the top of your machine and regular thread that matches the backing in the bobbin. A clear nylon thread is best for light fabrics; a darker, smoky color, for darker fabrics. If possible, use a walking foot on your machine. A regular presser foot tends to push the top layer ahead of the two bottom layers. The walking foot feeds all three layers under the needle at the same time.

Simply quilting in the ditch (between seams) is the easiest method for machine quilting, but intricate quilting can also be done by machine with a darning foot.

Binding

Finished bindings that are 3/8" wide appear more proportionate to tiny quilts than the more traditional 1/2" binding. It is not necessary to use bias bindings on quilts with straight sides.

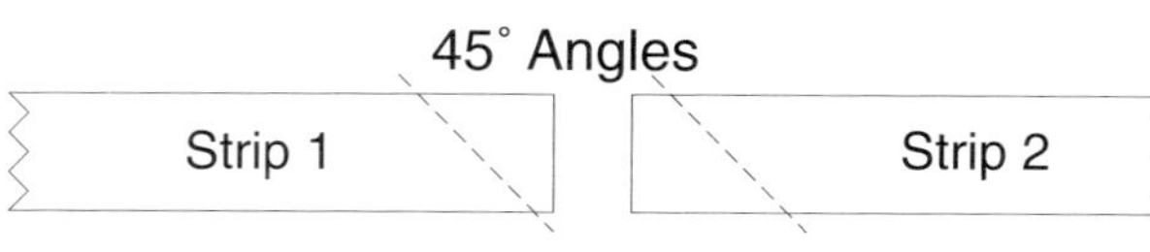

Measure the outer perimeter of the quilt to determine the total length of binding needed. Add about 8" more to this length to allow for mitering the corners and making the final joining of the binding. On the crossgrain of the fabric, cut enough 2" wide strips to total this measurement. Join the strips into one long strip by cutting the ends at a 45° angle and then sewing two angled edges together with a 1/4" seam. The seam will be almost unnoticeable because the bulk is distributed evenly. Join the two ends by extending each point 1/4" (seam allowance) and pin in place. Sew a 1/4" seam and press open (Fig. 29).

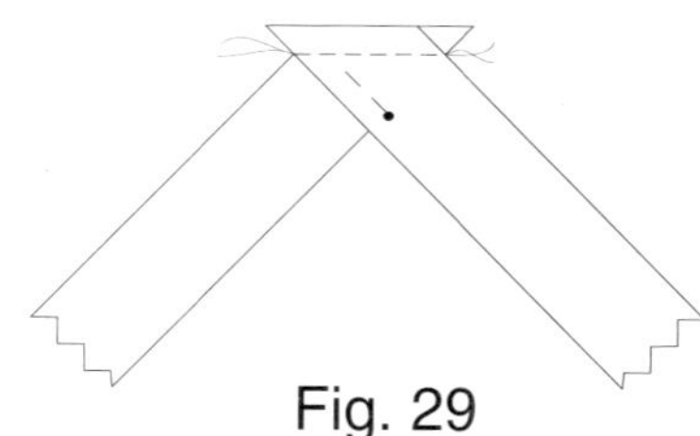
Fig. 29

With wrong sides together, press the joined strips in half lengthwise, making a 1" wide double binding strip.

Before applying the binding to the quilt, pin the quilt's edges as illustrated. Using the walking foot, sew a narrow seam all around the edges. This will result in a smooth, pucker-free bound edge. I also find it helpful not to cut off any of the excess batting and backing until after I have machine-sewn the binding onto the quilt (Fig. 30).

Replace the walking foot with the regular presser foot. Starting about one-fourth of the way up from the bottom right, lay the raw edges of the binding on the raw edges of the quilt top. Leave about 6" of the binding free behind the foot (for joining the ends later), and begin sewing down to the lower corner using a 1/4" seam. Stop stitching exactly 1/4" from the corner edge. Leave the needle in the fabric, raise the presser foot and turn the quilt so that you are ready to sew down the next edge. Backstitch one stitch and sew forward one stitch to secure the seam; clip the threads. Fold the binding straight up, forming a 45° angle, and then make a second fold just above the top edge of the quilt top. Make sure folded edges on the left are exactly aligned. Start sewing forward about 3/16" from the edge for several stitches, backstitch to secure, and sew forward again to the next corner (Fig. 31 and Fig. 32).

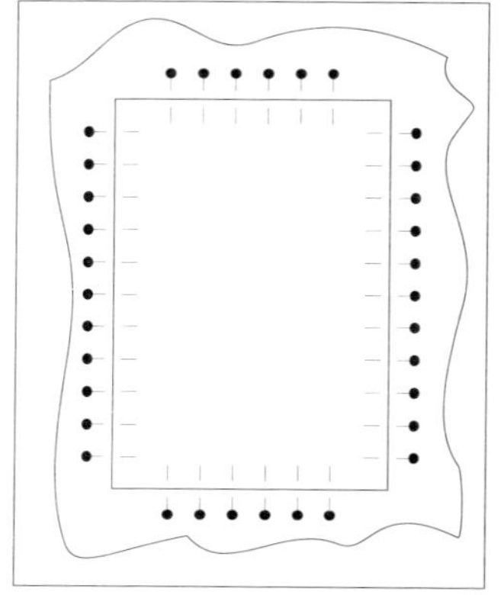
Fig. 30

Repeat this procedure for each corner. When you come back to the first side, stop stitching near the top of the quilt about one-fourth of the way down and backstitch. Remove the quilt from the machine and lay it on a flat surface. Lay the free ends of the binding along the unstitched portion of the quilt's edge and overlap them. Mark the left end with a pin at the midpoint of the unstitched portion of the binding. Open out the left end of the binding. Using the square ruler, cut a 45° angle at the pin mark (Fig. 33). Refold the strip.

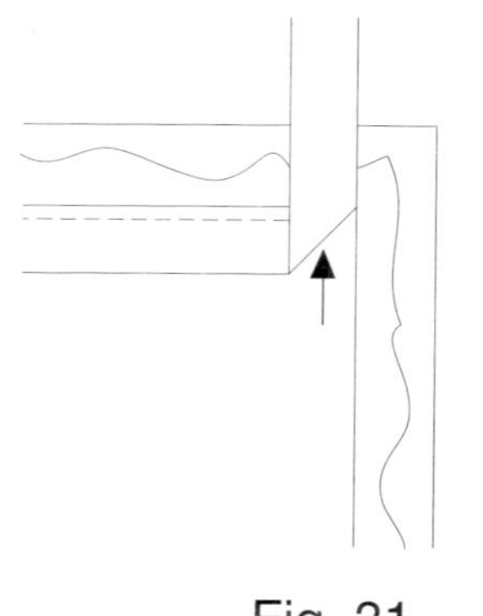
Fig. 31

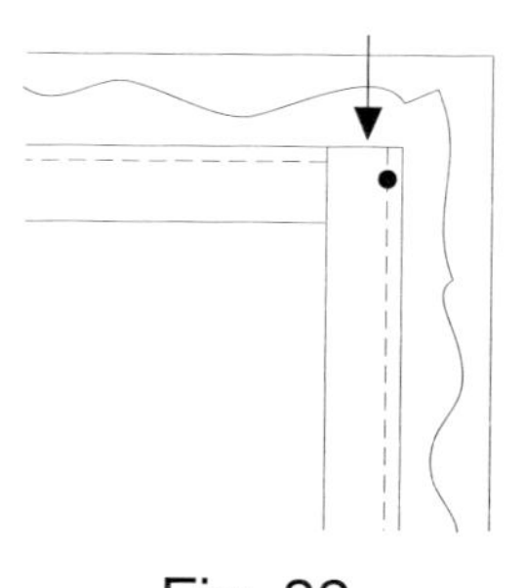
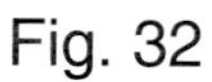
Fig. 32

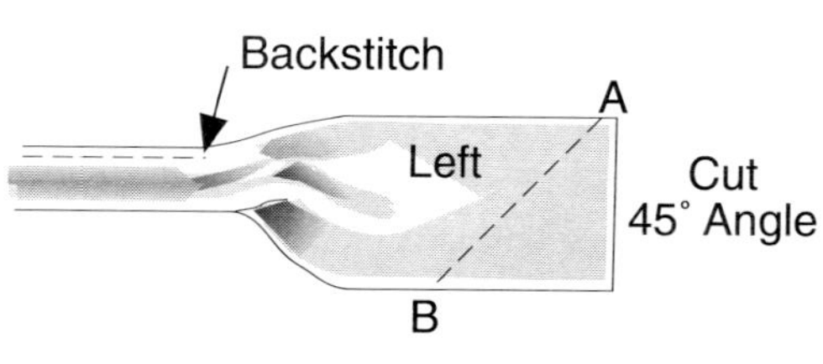

Fig. 33

Lay the unstitched left end over the right end. On the right end, mark points A and B with a dot (Fig. 34).

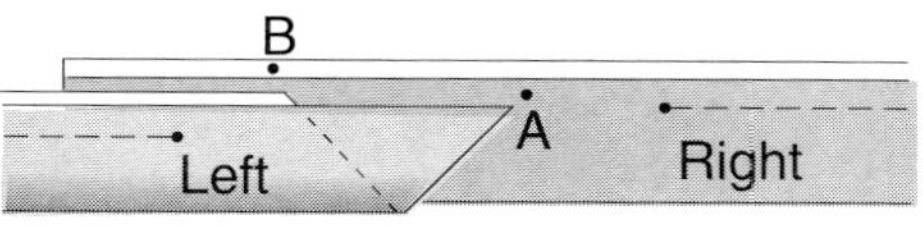

Fig. 34

Open out the right end. Measure and cut a 45° angle 1/2" to the left of the dots (Fig. 35).

Place the right sides of the two ends together and sew with a 1/4" seam allowance (Fig. 36). Press the seam open and fold the joined strip in half. Press. Lay the unstitched portion of the binding on the edge of the quilt top and finish sewing it to the quilt.

Now is the time to trim the excess batting and backing, about 1/4" from the edges of the quilt top. This allowance will fill the 3/8" binding completely. Wrap the binding over the edge to the back of the quilt. Place the folded edge of the binding on top of the stitching line and sew a tiny blindstitch to secure it. Your stitches should be no farther apart than 1/8".

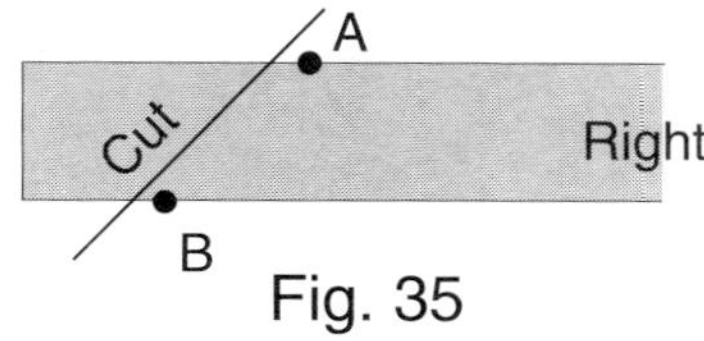

Fig. 35

The binding on the top of the quilt will already be mitered. On the back, fold the miter in the opposite direction from that on the front and secure it with tiny blindstitches (Fig. 37).

Signing Your Quilts

Do sign your quilts on the back! Include your name, city and state, and the year. You might wish to include the name of the quilt, that of the recipient and the occasion for the quilt's presentation. You can embroider the information onto the backing or onto a fabric label by hand or machine. You can create a counted cross-stitch label. Beautiful labels can be made by writing on muslin with a Micron Pigma 01 pen. These pens produce fine lines that do not bleed, wash out or fade. Labels can simply be typed on a piece of muslin that has been stabilized on the back with freezer paper.

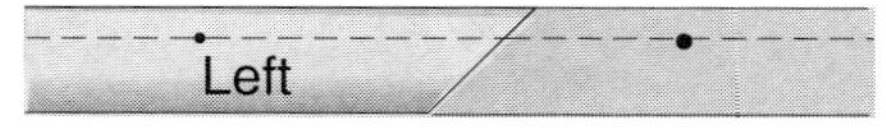

Fig. 36

Caring for Your Completed Quilts

Spraying finished quilts with fabric protector will help keep dirt from penetrating the fibers of the fabric. I use a soft bristle baby brush to remove lint and dust. If, at some time, a quilt requires laundering, simply wash it by hand in a basin of lukewarm water with Orvus Paste. Let it soak a short while, then gently squeeze the suds through it. Do not wring the quilt; just gently squeeze out the excess water and soap. Rinse thoroughly several times until no soap remains. Roll the quilt in a towel to absorb water, then allow it to dry flat on a clean towel or sweater dryer. If your quilt has a cotton batting, you may wish to partially tumble dry it to allow some shrinkage. This will cause some puckering to occur, which will give it more of an antique look.

If you must store your quilts, do not use plastic bags or boxes. Place the quilts in cotton pillowcases which allow the natural fibers to breathe. Quilts should be aired out occasionally and they should also be refolded to prevent permanent creases from forming.

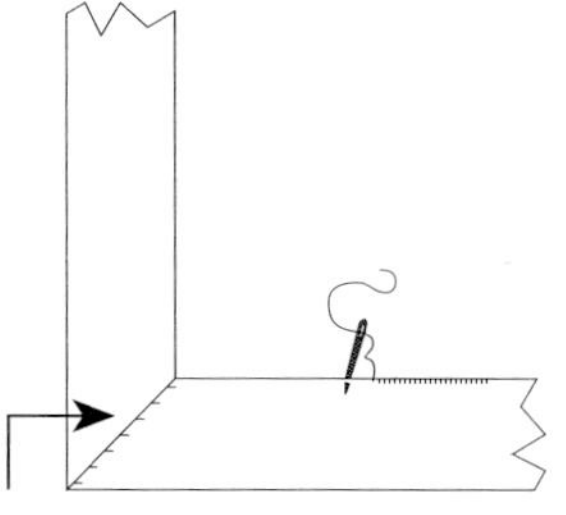
Blindstitch corners also

Fig. 37

With proper care, your Tiny Amish Traditions will become family heirlooms.

SHOO-FLY

quilt shown on page 30

8 1/2" x 10 1/2"
12 Pieced Blocks

Shoo-Fly is a favorite Amish pie. Because it is very sweet and gooey, it is said to attract flies.

The original 72" x 84" quilt containing 20 pieced blocks was made in Nappanee, Elkhart County, Indiana, in 1908. It is in the collection of Rebecca Haarer. My tiny version is very quick and easy to piece.

1 1/2"
Finished Blocks

Use 1/4" seam allowance; trim to 1/8" where needed to eliminate bulk.

FABRIC REQUIREMENTS

3/4 yard dark pink for background, second border and backing
3/8 yard medium gray for blocks, first border and binding
1/4 yard black for background of blocks

CUTTING AND PIECING

1. Make (48) 1" half-square triangle units of a black and medium gray combination.

Cut (1) 1 3/4" x 44" strip of black and (1) 1 3/4" x 44" strip of medium gray. Subcut each strip into (24) 1 3/4" squares. Draw a diagonal line on the back of the (24) gray squares. With right sides together, place a marked gray square on top of a black square and sew a 1/4" seam on one side of the marked diagonal line. HINT: Sewing these seams with a 1/8" seam will eliminate having to trim them back. Continue chain-piecing the seams of the remaining (23) units. Chain-piece 1/4" or 1/8" seams on the other side of the diagonal lines of all (24) units (Fig. 1). Clip units apart.

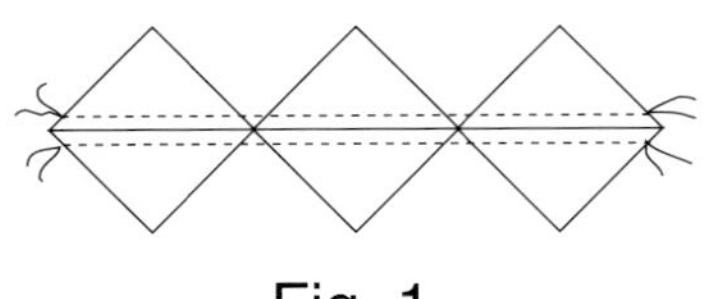

Fig. 1

Cut each unit in half on its diagonal line. Press seams to black fabric. Trim each square to 1" with a square ruler. Align the diagonal line of the square ruler on the unit's bias seam and cut the top two edges. Rotate the half-square triangle unit 180° and position the 1" lines of the square ruler on the first two cut edges. Make the last two cuts (Fig. 2). Trim seams to 1/8" if 1/4" seams were used.

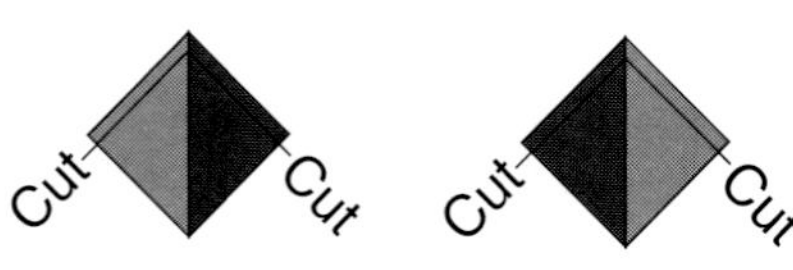

Fig. 2

2. Cut (2) 1" x 44" strips of black and subcut (24) 1" squares and (2) 1" x 13" strips.

3. Cut (1) 1" x 13" strip of gray.
4. Make (1) strip set-up of the 13" strips for Row 2 of the blocks (Fig. 3). Press seams toward the black. It is not necessary to trim these seams. Subcut (12) 1" segments.
5. Piece Rows 1 and 3 by chain-piecing units together (Fig. 4 and 5). Press seams toward the black.
6. Sew the rows together. Press seams toward the center row and trim to 1/8".

Fig. 3

ASSEMBLY
1. Cut (6) 2" squares of pink for alternate blocks.
2. Cut (3) 3 3/4" squares of pink and cut diagonally both ways to make (10) setting triangles.
3. Cut (2) 3 1/4" squares of pink and cut diagonally in half to make (4) corner triangles.
4. Lay out all the units in sequence. Sew the units into diagonal rows, and press seams away from the pieced blocks. Sew the rows together. Add the corners last.
Trim the setting triangles and corner triangles evenly around the assembled quilt top, leaving a 1/4" seam allowance.
5. First Border: Cut (1) 7/8" x 44" strip of gray. Subcut to fit and stitch to the quilt using the straight-cut corner method. Press seams toward the outside of the quilt.
6. Second Border: Cut (1) 1 3/4" x 44" strip of pink. Subcut to fit and stitch to the quilt using the straight-cut corner method. Press seams toward the outside of the quilt.
7. Layer the quilt with thin batting and pink backing.
8. Quilt as desired.
9. Finish the quilt with gray binding.

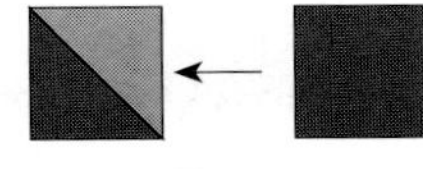
Fig. 4

Fig. 5

RAILROAD CROSSING (VARIATION) ——— quilt shown on page 30

12 1/2" x 16 1/2"

This pattern is not one of pieced blocks but rather of pieced sashing strips, which resemble railroad ties. The original quilt, dated March 5, 1943, was made in Denton, Ohio. It is in the collection of Judi Boisson Antique American Quilts, New York. Eighteen solid squares surrounded by the railroad tie strips make up that 66" x 84" quilt. My tiny version has only eight solid blocks with 1/4" strips in the sashing units for the railroad ties.

Use 1/4" seam allowance; trim to 1/8" where needed to eliminate bulk.

FABRIC REQUIREMENTS

1 yard medium blue for background, second border, backing and binding
1/8 yard light pink
1/8 yard bright royal blue
1/8 yard dark green
1/8 yard bright red
1/8 yard light green
1/8 yard blue (not background blue)

CUTTING

1. Medium Blue Blocks (Need 8)
Cut (1) 2 3/4" x 23" strip and subcut (8) 2 3/4" squares.
2. Medium Blue Setting Triangles (Need 6)
Cut (2) 4 3/4" squares and cut both ways diagonally.
3. Medium Blue Corner Triangles (Need 4)
Cut (2) 4 1/2" squares and cut in half diagonally.
4. Royal Blue Squares (Need 7)
Cut (1) 1 1/4" x 10" strip and subcut (7) 1 1/4" squares.
5. Royal Blue Setting Triangles (Need 10)
Cut (3) 2 3/4" squares and cut both ways diagonally.
6. Nine-Strip Railroad Ties (Need 24 units)
Cut the following number of 3/4" x 44" strips:
(2) bright red
(2) light pink
(2) dark green
(2) light green
(1) blue (not background blue)
Cut each of the strips into (2) 20" lengths. This will make it easier to sew and press the nine-strip set-ups.

PIECING OF NINE-STRIP UNITS

1. Make (2) set-ups as illustrated (Fig. 1). Sew strips together lengthwise. Press seams in one direction. They will be trimmed later.
2. Subcut (12) 1 1/4" wide units from each set-up.

Light Pink
Dark Green
Light Green
Bright Red
Blue
Bright Red
Light Green
Dark Green
Light Pink

Fig. 1

ASSEMBLY

1. Lay out the units in sequence on a flat surface. It is helpful to have a stabilizer underneath the units, such as a piece of flannel, felt or terry cloth.
2. Sew the units into diagonal rows. The nine-strip units must fit the adjoining 2 3/4" squares. First correct any of the 1/4" seams of the nine-strip unit to make it fit the adjoining square. After adjustments are made, trim each seam in the unit to 1/8". The setting triangles and corner triangles are oversized. Let the outer sides of these triangles extend beyond the other units. Press seams away from the nine-strip units.
3. Sew the rows together. Add the corners last.
4. Trim the setting triangles and corner triangles evenly around the quilt, leaving a 1/4" seam allowance.
5. First Border: Cut (2) 1" x 44" strips of light pink. Subcut to fit and sew to the quilt using the straight-cut corner method. Press the seams toward the outside of the quilt.
6. Second Border: Cut (2) 2" x 44" strips of background blue. Subcut to fit and sew to the quilt using the straight-cut corner method. Press the seams toward the outside of the quilt.
7. Layer the quilt with thin batting and blue backing.
8. Quilt as desired.
9. Finish the quilt with blue binding.

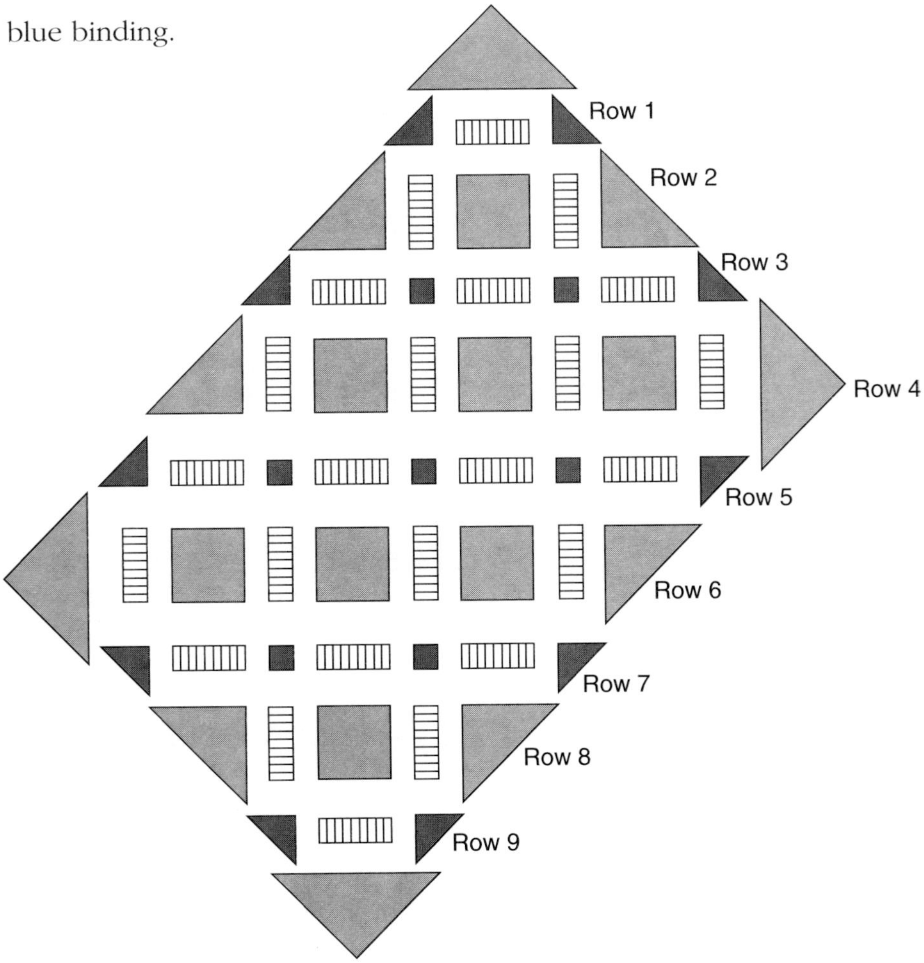

Row 1
Row 2
Row 3
Row 4
Row 5
Row 6
Row 7
Row 8
Row 9

CUPS AND SAUCERS IN A GARDEN MAZE

quilt shown on page 33

12 1/2" x 16"
6 Pieced Blocks

This is the first miniature Amish quilt that I made. A picture of the original 68" x 83" quilt, containing 24 pieced blocks, made me eager to try a tiny version. The lovely Garden Maze setting could be a challenge to piece in miniature, but I have simplified the method for the intersecting corner blocks. The original masterpiece was made in 1919, in La Grange County, Indiana. It is now in the collection of Rebecca Haarer of Shipshewana, Indiana.

Use 1/4 " seam allowance; trim to 1/8" where needed to eliminate bulk.

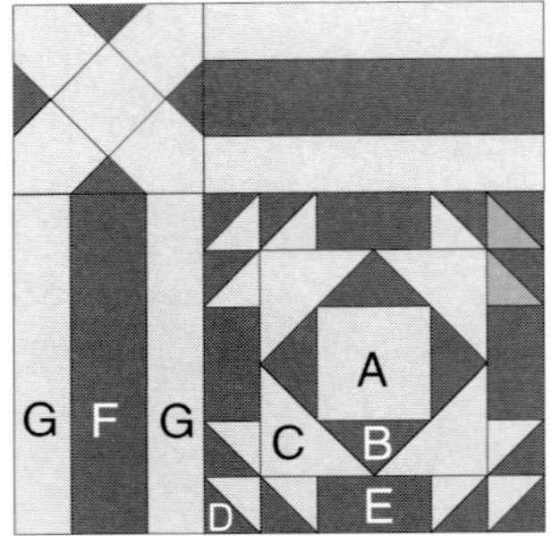

2 1/4" Finished Blocks

FABRIC REQUIREMENTS
3/4 yard light red for blocks, sashing, second border and backing
1/2 yard medium green for blocks, sashing and binding
1/8 yard dark red for first border

CUTTING AND PIECING OF BLOCKS (Letters correspond to the block diagram)

A. Cut (1) 1 1/4" x 8" strip of green. Subcut (6) 1 1/4" squares for centers of blocks.

B. Cut (1) 1 3/4" x 22" strip of light red. Subcut (12) 1 3/4" squares. Cut squares diagonally in half to make (24) corner triangles. These triangles are oversized and will be trimmed later.

1. Sew corner triangles to two opposite sides of each center square (Fig. 1). Press the seams toward the center squares. Trim seams.

2. Sew triangles to the remaining two sides of center squares (Fig. 2). Press the seams away from the center squares. Trim seams.

3. Trim each unit to a 1 3/4" square. Align the diagonal line on the square ruler with the center of a unit and trim the top two sides, leaving a 1/4" seam allowance. Turn the unit around and line up the two sides that were just cut with the 1 3/4" square lines on the ruler and cut third and fourth sides. Be sure to leave a 1/4" seam allowance from all four corners of the center square (Fig. 3).

C. Cut (12) 2" squares of green. Cut diagonally in half to make (24) corner triangles. Sew these triangles to the A/B units following the steps given under (B). Trim seams. Trim all units to 2" squares, leaving a 1/4" seam allowance from all corners of the previous units.

D. Make (72) 7/8" half-square triangle units of a light red and green combination, as follows.

Fig. 1

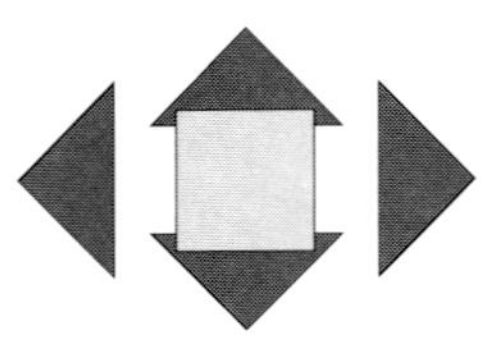
Fig. 2

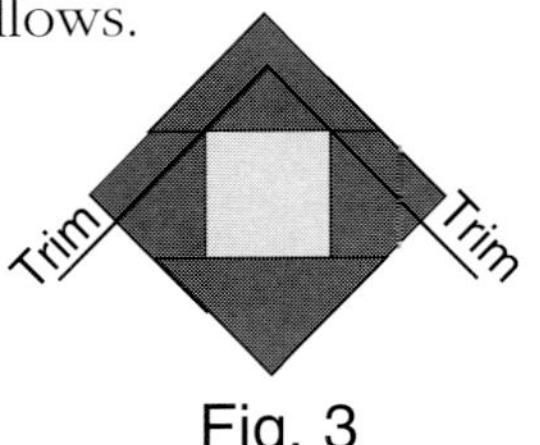

Fig. 3

1. Cut (2) 1 3/4" x 44" strips of light red and of green. Subcut (36) 1 3/4" squares from each fabric color. Draw a diagonal line on the back of the (36) green squares. With right sides together, place a marked green square on top of a light red square and sew a 1/4" seam on one side of the marked diagonal line.

HINT: Sewing these seams with a 1/8" seam will eliminate having to trim them back. Continue chain-piecing the seams of the remaining (35) units. Chain-piece 1/4" or 1/8" seams on the other side of the diagonal lines of all (36) units. Clip units apart (Fig. 4).

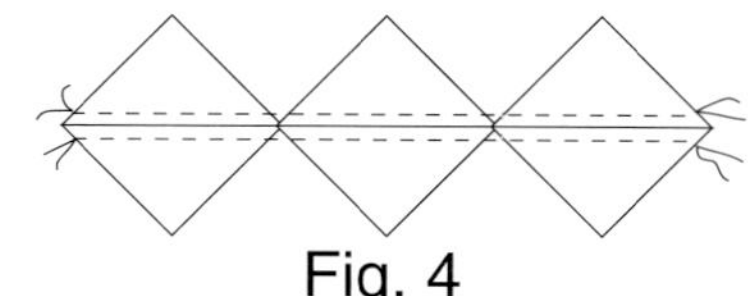
Fig. 4

2. Cut each unit in half on its diagonal line. Press seams to the green fabric.

3. Trim each square to 7/8" with a square ruler. Align the diagonal line of a square ruler on the unit's bias seam and cut the top two edges. Rotate the half-square triangle unit 180° and position the 7/8" lines of the square ruler on the first two cut edges. Make the last two cuts (Fig. 5). Trim seams to 1/8" if 1/4" seams were used.

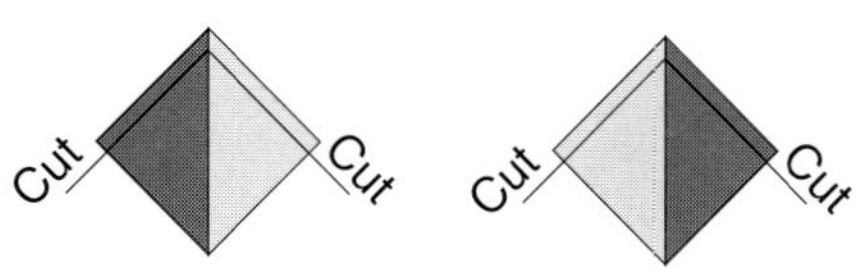

Fig. 5

E. Cut (1) 7/8" x 44" strip of light red. Subcut (24) 7/8" x 1 1/4" rectangles.

ASSEMBLY OF BLOCKS

1. Chain-piece (24) units. Press the seams toward the rectangles. Trim the seams (Fig. 6).

Fig. 6

2. Sew a half-square triangle unit to each end of (12) of the above units. Press the seams toward the rectangles. Trim the seams (Fig. 7).

3. Assemble all the units into six blocks (Fig. 8 and Fig. 9). Press the seams away from the centers.

Fig. 7

CUTTING AND PIECING OF SASHING FOR GARDEN MAZE

Need (17) units.

F. Cut (1) 1" x 44" strip of light red plus (1) 1" x 6" strip.

G. Cut (2) 7/8" x 44" strips of green plus (1) 7/8" x 12" strip. Cut the 12" strip into (2) 6" segments. Sew the long red strip between the two long green strips lengthwise (Fig. 10). Repeat for the short strips. Press the seams toward the green. Subcut (17) 2 3/4" units. Trim the seams.

CUTTING AND PIECING THE CORNER UNITS FOR THE GARDEN MAZE (Fig. 11). Need (12) units.

NOTE: Because of the diminutive size of these units (1 1/4" finished size), I have pieced Nine Patch units from bias strips and cut the units on the diagonal with a square ruler to the exact size needed. The

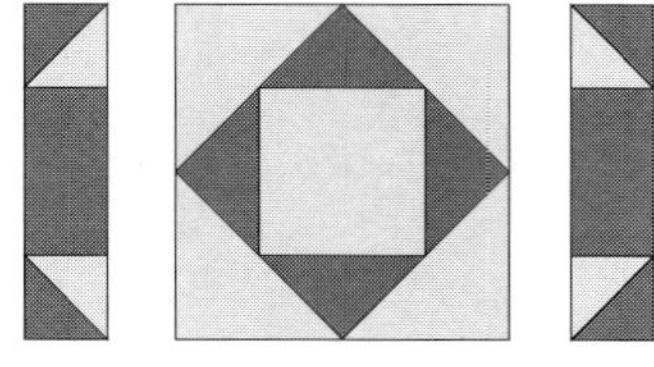
Fig. 8

Fig. 9

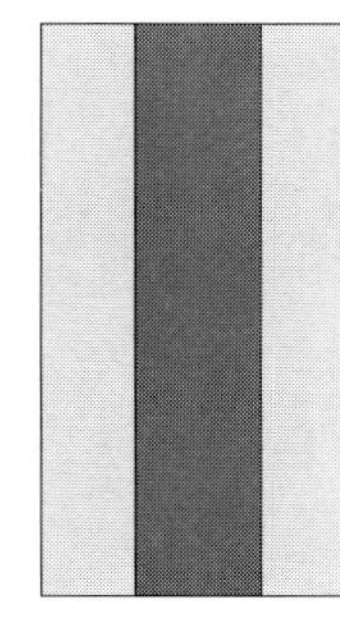
Fig. 10

Fig. 11

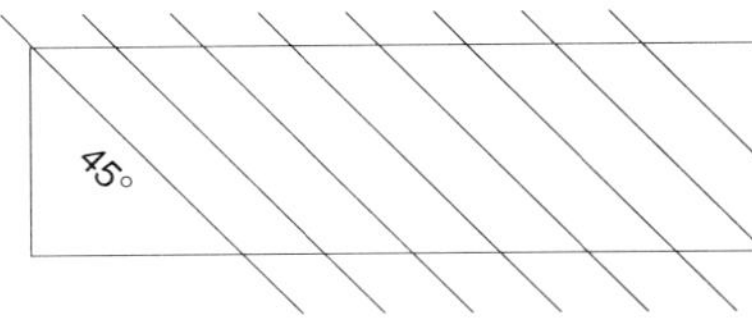

Fig. 12

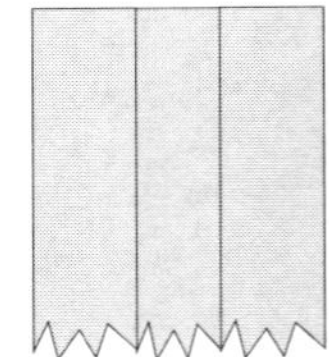

Fig. 13
1 3/8" - 1" - 1 3/8"
Make (2) set-ups
Press seams away from center

Fig. 14
1 3/8" - 1" - 1 3/8"
Make (4) set-ups
Press seams toward center

straight-of-grain will be on the outside of the units (Fig. 12).

1. Cut (6) 1" x 9" bias strips of green.
2. Cut (4) 1 3/8" x 9" bias strips of green.
3. Cut (8) 1 3/8" x 9" bias strips of light red.
4. Sew these bias strips into set-ups for Nine Patch units (Fig. 13 and Fig. 14).
5. Subcut the first (2) set-ups into (12) 1" segments. Subcut the second (4) set-ups into (24) 1 3/8" segments.
6. Make (12) Nine Patch units (Fig. 15). Press the seams away from the center.
7. With square ruler cut the bias Nine Patch units on the diagonal to 1 3/4" units (Fig. 16).

ASSEMBLY

1. Sew the quilt units into seven rows according to the picture of the quilt. Press the seams toward the strips (Fig. 17 and Fig. 18).
2. Sew the rows together. Press the seams toward the sashing strips.
3. First Border: Cut (1) 1" x 44" strip of dark red. Subcut to fit and stitch to the quilt using the straight-cut corner method. Press the seams toward the outside of the quilt.
4. Second Border: Cut (2) 2 1/4" x 44" strips of light red. Subcut to fit and stitch to the quilt using the straight-cut corner method. Press the seams toward the outside of the quilt.
5. Layer the quilt with thin batting and light red backing.
6. Quilt as desired.
7. Finish off quilt with green binding.

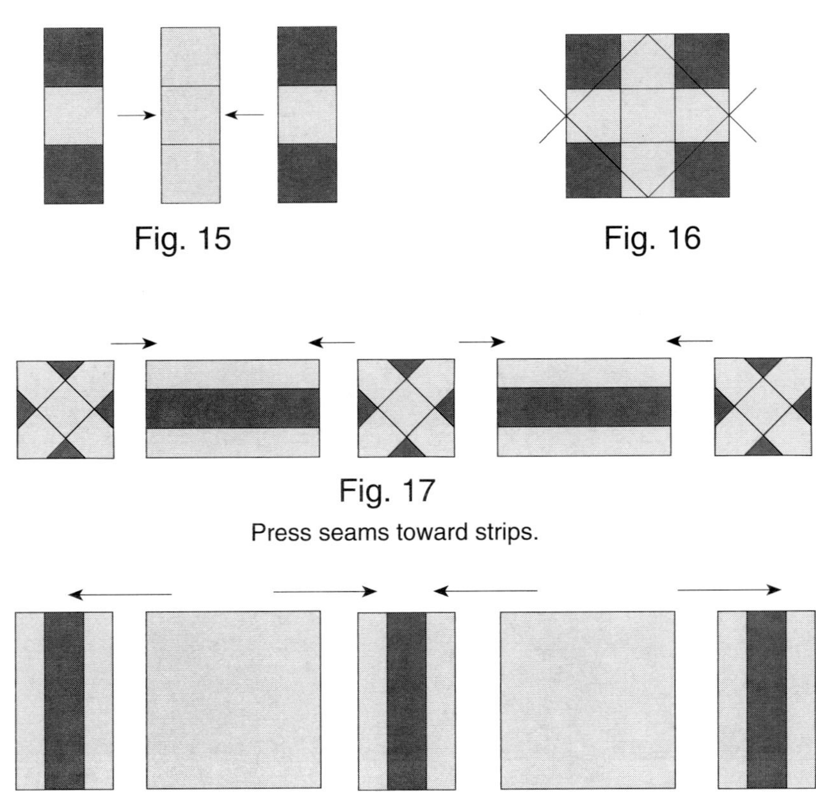

Fig. 15

Fig. 16

Fig. 17
Press seams toward strips.

Fig. 18
Press seams toward strips.

Get out your solid fabric scraps for this "**Rail Fence**" (12" x 13", left). Three narrow borders give this quilt a crisp, finished look. Pattern on page 52.

A dozen pink pinwheels spin merrily in **Crazy Ann** (10 5/8" x 13", on the wall). It's so easy to piece from trimmed down Flying Geese units. Pattern on page 44.

Try this "**Tumbling Blocks**" (11" x 12 1/2", right). It is easier than you might think. No set-in seams! Pattern on page 58.

Shoo-Fly is an Amish favorite for two good reasons—it's a pie and a quilt pattern! This "**Shoo-Fly**" (8 1/2" x 10 1/2", left and facing page) features a dozen blocks set on point. Pattern on page 22.

Eight "magic fingers" are the secret to perfect curved piecing in this "**Drunkard's Path**" (15" square, on the wall). A narrow Sawtooth inner border is a geometric complement. Pattern on page 37.

Lay down tracks as you piece this "**Railroad Crossing (Variation)**" (12 1/2" x 16 1/2", right and facing page). Pieced sashing strips add plenty of excitement to the simple blocks. Pattern on page 24.

"**Shoo-Fly**"

Simple lines and unadorned surfaces characterize Amish quilts. Jewel-tone colors used in the six fan blades make this "**Fan**" (10" x 12") a perfect Tiny Amish Tradition! Pattern on page 46.

"**Railroad Crossing (Variation)**"

Violet sashing strips with pink cornerstones give the impression that you are viewing this "**Barn Raising**" quilt (15" square) through a window. Pattern on page 40.

"**Cups and Saucers in a Garden Maze**"

Facing Page:
A narrow border frames 12 spinning pinwheels. "**Pinwheel (Variation)**" (10 1/2" x 12 1/2", top) is easy to stitch using pieced bias strips. Pattern on page 56.

The half-square triangle units in "**Crown of Thorns**" (11" x 15", right) are quick-pieced. Six blocks are set off with a triple border. Pattern on page 54.

Simplified piecing for the corner blocks makes this setting a breeze in "**Cups and Saucers in a Garden Maze**" (12 1/2" x 16', on the floor). Pattern on page 26.

Wilkum

WELCOME

A full-size quilt made in Ohio inspired this tiny "**Lone Star**" (15 1/2" square). Strip-piecing makes handling the 288 mini diamonds a lot more manageable. Pattern on page 62.

Facing Page:
This miniature "**Bow Tie**" quilt (15 1/4" x 16 1/4", on the wall, left) contains more than 600 pieces! See how simple it is to make—with no set-in seams. Pattern on page 42.

An Amish crib quilt, circa 1900, was the inspiration for this mini version of "**Amish Baskets**" (11" x 13", on the wall, right). Pattern on page 50.

Two of the best known Amish quilt patterns, Sunshine and Shadow and Diamond in a Square, are cleverly combined in this "**Sunshine and Shadow**" (14" square, on the chair). This tiny version contains 3/8" finished squares in eight different colors. Pattern on page 60.

"**Sunshine and Shadow**"

The full-size version of this 1920s Indiana quilt has only one blue block that retained its original color. Piece your mini "**Jacob's Ladder**" (14 1/2" x 19") the same way to reflect its history. Pattern on page 48.

quilt shown on page 30

DRUNKARD'S PATH

15" Square

This traditional pattern first appeared in Ladies Art Company Catalogue *in 1898. Because of the resemblance to puzzle pieces, it is also know as Solomon's Puzzle. In I Kings 3:16-28, King Solomon displayed great wisdom in dealing with a seemingly unsolvable puzzle. The Amish would no doubt prefer this Biblical name.*

The original Amish quilt is 80" x 84" and was made in 1920-30, in Withee, Wisconsin. Judi Boisson Antique American Quilts, New York, owns the beautiful quilt. My miniature version contains 121 pieced squares just as the original does, but has 92 half-square triangle units in the first border rather than 106.

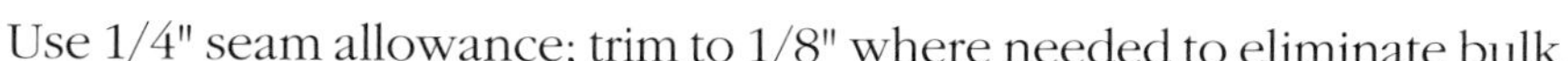

Use 1/4" seam allowance; trim to 1/8" where needed to eliminate bulk.

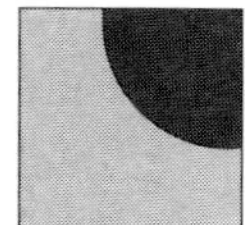

Make (60)

NOTE: Piecing this pattern is considered a challenge reserved for advanced quilters. Machine piecing 1" finished squares could be very difficult. I tried different methods and was not satisfied with the results. Maybe appliqué would be the easiest method. Then I discovered what worked for me. It is not only easy but fast!

FABRIC REQUIREMENTS

1 1/8 yards light green for piecing, second border and backing
3/4 yard bright red for piecing and binding

Make (61)
1" Finished
Squares

TEMPLATES

Make (3) templates. Trace A, B and C onto template plastic and cut them out on the inside of the traced lines.

CUTTING INSTRUCTIONS

1. Light Green Fabric
   Need (60) L-shapes (Fig. 1).

Cut (2) 1 1/2" x 44" strips. Keep each strip folded in four layers. Cut a straight edge at the selvage ends of the first layered strip. Subcut (7) 1 1/2" cuts, making a total of (28) 1 1/2" squares (Fig. 2). Keep squares in piles of four layers. On the top square of each pile, fit the (A) Template into the square and trace the curve. Cut the pie shape out of four layers at the same time with a sharp pair of scissors. Repeat for the other strip. Cut (4) more 1 1/2" squares and remove the pie shapes. Discard the pie shapes.

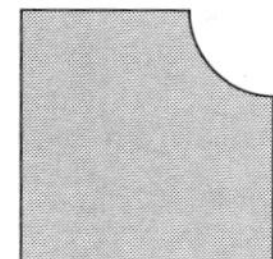

Fig. 1

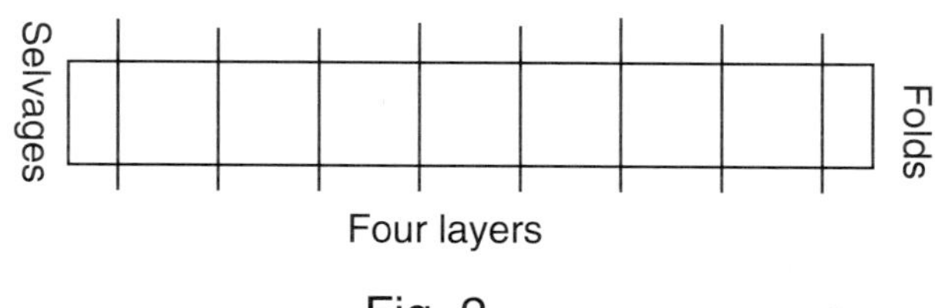

Fig. 2

2. Bright Red Fabric
   Need (61) L-shapes (Fig. 3).

Cut (2) 1 1/2" x 44" strips. Follow the instructions for the light green

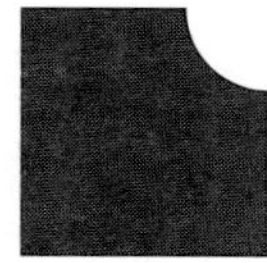

Fig. 3

L-shapes. Cut (5) more 1 1/2" squares and cut out the pie shapes.

3. Light Green Fabric
   Need (61) Pie Shapes (Fig. 4).

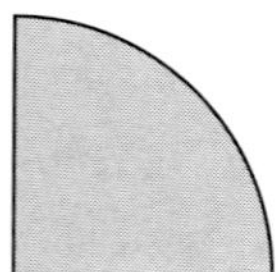
Fig. 4

Cut (2) 1 1/4" x 44" strips. Keep each strip folded in four layers. Cut a straight edge at the selvage ends of the first layered strip. Subcut (8) 1 1/4" cuts, making a total of (32) 1 1/4" squares. Keep squares in piles of four layers. On the top square of each pile, fit the (C) template into the square and trace the curve. Cut the curve on all four layers at the same time. Repeat for the other strip. Discard the remainders.

4. Bright Red Fabric
   Need (60) Pie Shapes (Fig. 5).

Fig. 5

Cut (2) 1 1/4" x 44" strips. Follow instructions for the light green pie shapes.

PIECING INSTRUCTIONS

1. Place Template (B) on the wrong side of each L-shape and trace the curve for the sewing line.

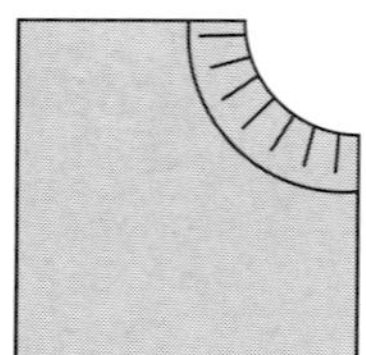
Fig. 6

2. With a sharp-pointed pair of scissors, make small clips into the seam allowance of the L-shapes. Stop short of the sewing line (Fig. 6). Make 7 evenly spaced clips into the seam allowance.

3. Place a dab of glue stick on the right side of each clipped section of the seam allowance. Finger press the sections at each end to the right side of the pie shape. Evenly space and finger press the other sections to the pie shape (Fig. 7). Glue green L-shapes to red pie shapes and red L-shapes to green pie shapes.

HINT: I glue about 20 units at one time and then chain-piece them on their sewing lines.

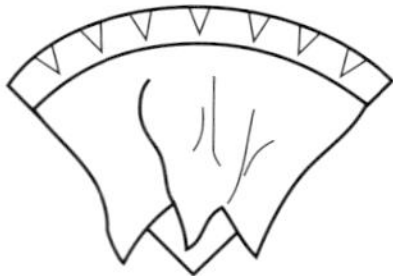
Fig. 7

4. Chain-piece these curved seams on the sewing lines. It's like having eight magic fingers holding the seam allowance in the right place. Press seams toward the L-shapes.

ASSEMBLY

1. Sew the square units into 11 rows according to the photo of the quilt. Press all seams of a row in one direction. Alternate the direction of the seams for each row. You do not need to trim these seams.

2. Sew rows together. Press seams downwards.

Fig. 8

3. First Border: Make (92) 1" half-square triangle units of a bright red and light green combination (Fig. 8). Cut (2) 1 3/4" x 44" strips of each fabric. Subcut (46) 1 3/4" squares of each color. Draw a diagonal line on the back of all the light green squares. With right sides together, place a marked green square on top of a red square and sew a 1/4" seam on one side of the marked diagonal line.

HINT: Sewing these seams with a 1/8" seam will eliminate having to trim them back. Continue chain-piecing the seams of the remaining (45) units. Chain-piece 1/4" or 1/8" seams on the other side of the diagonal lines of all (46) units. Clip units apart (Fig. 9).

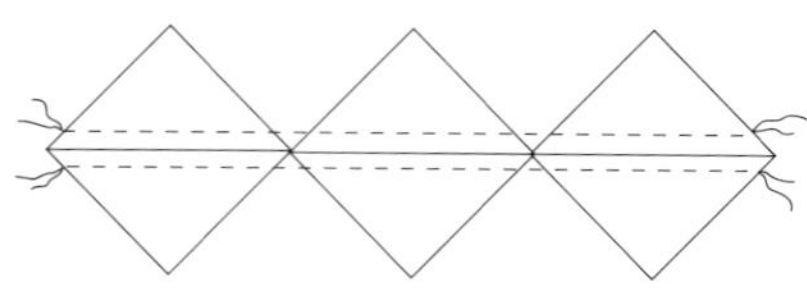
Fig. 9

Cut each unit in half on its diagonal line. Press the seams toward the red fabric. Trim each square to 1" with a square ruler. Align the diagonal line of the square ruler on the unit's bias seam and cut the top two edges. Rotate the half-square triangle unit 180° and position the 1" lines of the square ruler on the first two cut edges. Make the last two cuts (Fig. 10). Trim the seams to 1/8" if 1/4" seams were used.

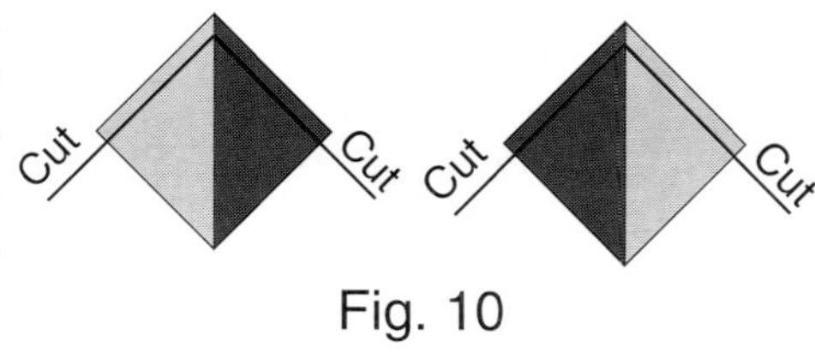

Fig. 10

Sew (2) strips of (22) half-square triangle units each for the side borders. Press the seams of the left border toward the green fabric. Trim the seams. Sew to the left side of the quilt top, fitting two half-square triangle units to each 1" Drunkard's Path unit. If necessary, adjust the seams of the half-square triangle units to fit the Drunkard's Path units. Press the seams of the right border toward the red fabric. Trim the seams and sew to the right side of the quilt. Press the border seams to the outside of the quilt.

Sew (2) strips of (24) half-square triangle units each for the top and bottom borders. Press the seams of the top border in the opposite direction of those in the first row of the quilt top. Trim the seams and sew to the top of the quilt. Press the seams of the bottom border in the opposite direction of those in the last row of the quilt top. Trim the seams and sew to the bottom of the quilt. Press border seams to the outside of the quilt.

4. Second Border: Cut (2) 2" x 44" strips of green. Divide each strip in half and sew to the first borders, mitering corners (refer to Borders section). Be very careful not to cut off the points of the half-square triangle units when adding this second border. Press the seams toward the outside of the quilt.
5. Layer the quilt with thin batting and light green backing.
6. Quilt as desired.
7. Finish the quilt with bright red binding.

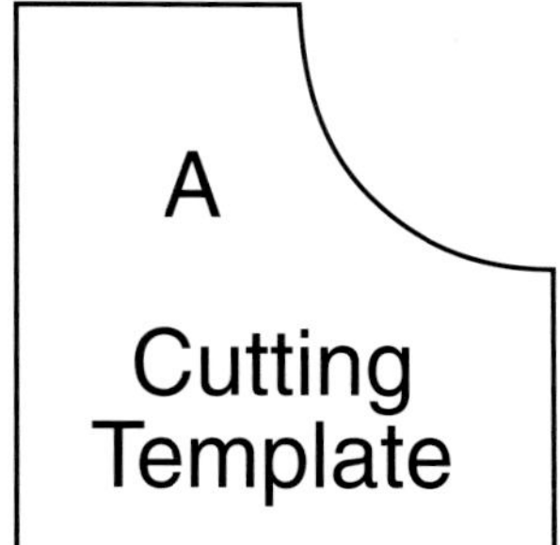

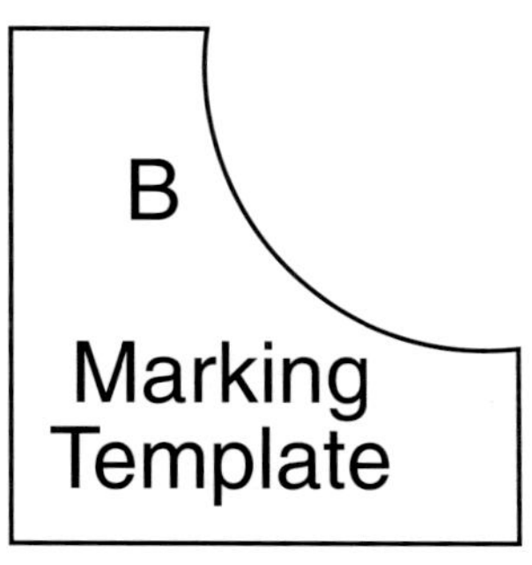

C

BARN RAISING DESIGN

quilt shown on page 32

Barn Raising Design
15" Square

This design has borrowed the Barn Raising set of the Log Cabin. Because of sashing strips, it resembles a Barn Raising quilt viewed through window panes. The original 74" x 78" quilt was made in Ohio, c. 1920, and is in the collection of Bryce and Donna Hamilton. My miniature version contains the same number of pieces as that large quilt and is quite easy to cut and piece.

Use 1/4" seam allowance; trim to 1/8" where needed to eliminate bulk.

FABRIC REQUIREMENTS

1 yard taupe for sashing, first border and backing
1/4 yard black for Barn Raising units
1/4 yard medium pink (blue tone) for Barn Raising units
1/8 yard purple (blue tone) for sashing
1/8 yard violet for sashing
1/8 yard bright pink for sashing
1/8 yard pink (peach tone) for sashing

CUTTING AND PIECING OF BARN RAISING UNITS

1. Cut (1) 1 1/2" square of medium pink for center.

2. Make (36) 1 1/2" half-square triangle units of a black and medium pink combination (Fig. 1). Cut (1) 2 1/4" x 44" strip of each fabric, and subcut (18) 2 1/4" squares of each color. Draw a diagonal line on the back of each medium pink square. With right sides together, place a marked medium pink square on top of a black square and sew a 1/4" seam on one side of the marked diagonal line. HINT: Sewing these seams with a 1/8" seam will eliminate having to trim them back. Continue chain-piecing the seams of the remaining (17) units. Chain-piece 1/4" or 1/8" seams on the other side of the diagonal line of all (18) units. (Fig. 2). Cut each unit in half on its diagonal line. Press seams to the black fabric. Trim each square to 1 1/2" with a square ruler. Align diagonal line of square ruler on the unit's bias seam and cut the top two edges. Rotate the half-square triangle unit 180° and position the 1 1/2" lines of the square ruler on the first two cut edges. Make the last two cuts (Fig. 3). Trim the seams to 1/8" if 1/4" seams were used.

3. Cut (1) 1" x 44" strip of medium pink and subcut (24) 1" x 1 1/2" rectangles. Cut (1) 1" x 44" strip of black and subcut (24) 1" squares. Draw a diagonal line on the wrong side of each black square, or press in a diagonal crease. Sew these squares on the diagonal to one end of each rectangle as illustrated (Fig. 4). Press each square over its seamline to the corner. Trim the two lower layers (the seam allowance) to 1/8". Sew (8) of these units into (4) pairs (Fig. 5). Press the center seam open.

4. Cut (1) 1" x 44" strip of black and subcut (28) 1" x 1 1/2" rectangles. Cut (1) 1" x 44" strip of medium pink and subcut (32) 1" squares. Draw a diagonal line on the wrong side of each medium pink square, or press in a diagonal crease. Sew (24) of these squares on the diagonal to one end of (24) rectangles as illustrated (Fig. 6). Press each square over its seamline to the corner. Trim the two lower layers (the seam allowance)

Fig. 1

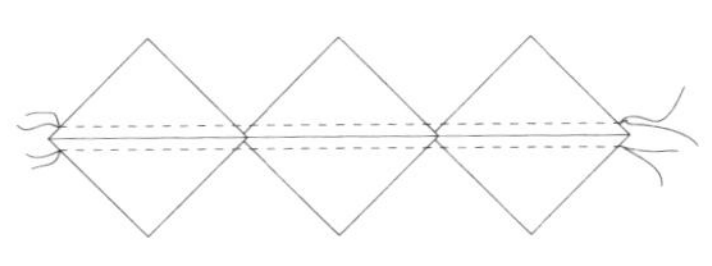

Fig. 2

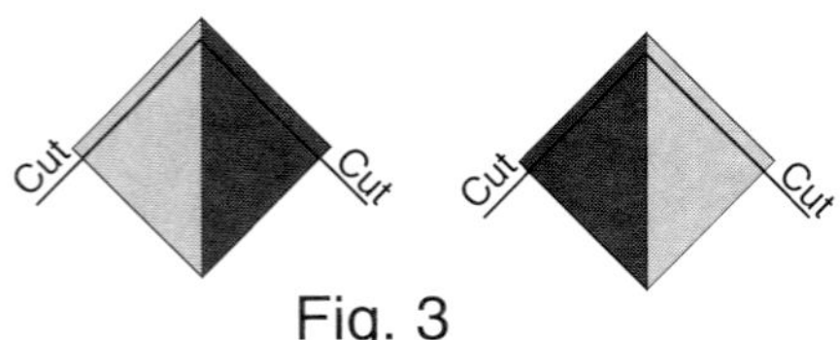

Fig. 3

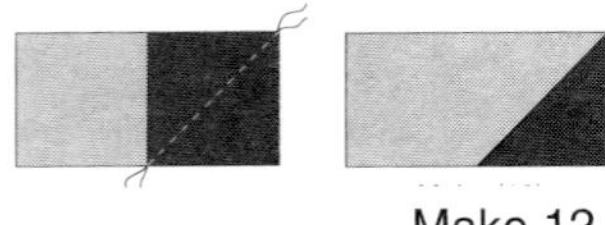

Make 12

Make 12

Fig. 4

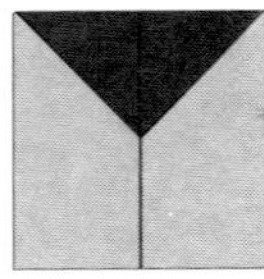

Make 4

Fig. 5

to 1/8". Sew (16) of these units into (8) pairs (Fig. 7). Press the center seam open. Make (4) Flying Geese units using the connector corner method described on page 12 (Fig. 8).

5. Cut (4) 1" squares of black.

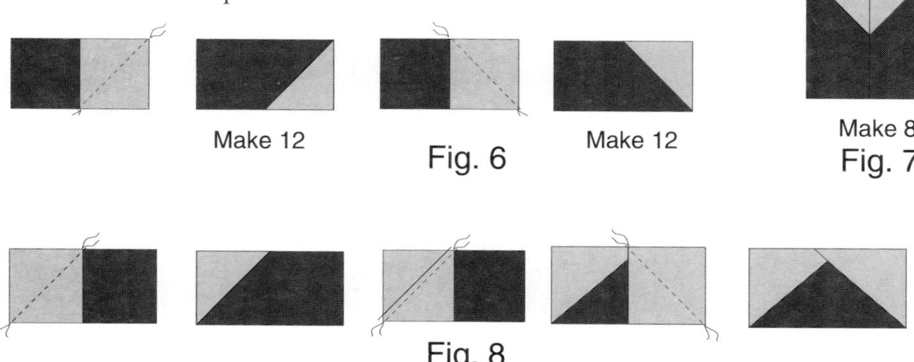

Fig. 6

Fig. 7

Fig. 8

CUTTING OF SASHING STRIPS

1. Taupe: Cut (3) 1" x 44" strips and subcut (56) 1" x 1 1/2" rectangles and (16) 1" squares.
2. Purple: Cut (2) 1" x 44" strips and subcut (35) 1" x 1 1/2" rectangles and (15) 1" squares.
3. Violet: Cut (1) 1" x 44" strip and subcut (21) 1" x 1 1/2" rectangles and (1) 1" square.
4. Bright Pink: Cut (1) 1" x 44" strip and subcut (41) 1" squares.
5. Pink (peach tone): Cut (1) 1" x 44" strip and subcut (23) 1" squares.

ASSEMBLY

1. Using the photograph of the quilt as your guide, lay out all the units and sashing sections in correct sequence on a flat surface. It is helpful to have a stabilizer underneath the layout, such as a piece of flannel, felt or terry cloth.
2. Sew the pieces into (17) rows. Press the seams of the odd-numbered rows toward the squares. Trim the seams. Press the seams of the even-numbered rows toward the rectangles. These seams do not need to be trimmed (Fig. 9).

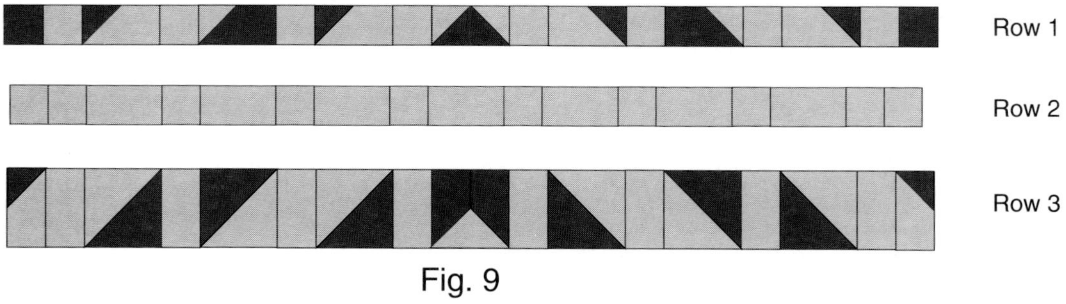

Fig. 9

3. Sew the rows together. Press the seams from the center toward the outside of the quilt.
4. First Border: Cut (2) 2 1/4" x 44" strips of taupe. Subcut to fit and sew to the quilt using the straight-cut corner method. Press the seams toward the outside of the quilt.
5. Layer the quilt with a thin batting and taupe backing.
6. Quilt as desired.
7. Finish the quilt with taupe binding.

BOW TIE

quilt shown on page 34

15 1/4" x 16 1/4"

This miniature Bow Tie quilt contains more than 600 pieces, just like the original 72" x 79" Amish quilt made in Ohio in 1930. Bryce and Donna Hamilton own that wonderful quilt. You can make this tiny version by using the connector corner method to make the centers of the bows. The method is easy, but you must follow the photo of the quilt to get the same color arrangement.

Use 1/4" seam allowance; trim to 1/8" where needed to eliminate bulk.

FABRIC REQUIREMENTS

3/4 yard ecru for background, second border and backing
1/4 yard black for units, first border and binding (Color A)
1/4 yard peach pink for units (Color B)
1/8 yard green for units (Color C)
1/8 yard dark plum for units (Color D)
1/8 yard royal blue for units (Color E)
1/8 yard bright pink for units (Color F)

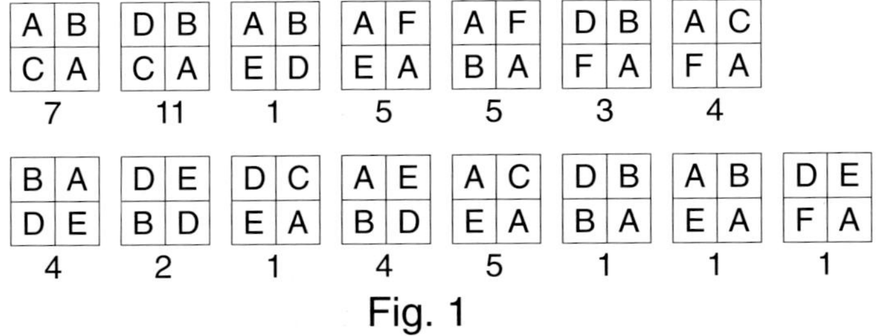

Fig. 1

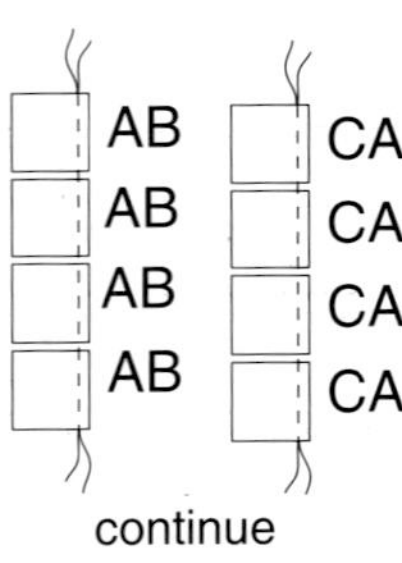

Fig. 2

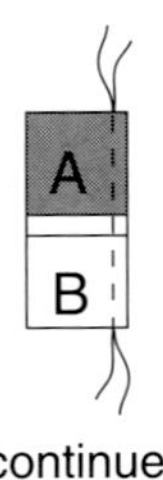

Fig. 3

CUTTING INSTRUCTIONS

Ecru Fabric

Cut (2) 1 1/2" x 44" strips. Subcut (55) 1 1/2" squares.

Cut (1) 1" x 44" strip. Subcut (21) 1" x 1 1/2" rectangles and (2) 1" squares.

Black Fabric (Color A)

Cut (3) 1" x 44" strips. Subcut (90) 1" squares.

Cut (2) 3/4" x 44" strips. Subcut (90) 3/4" squares.

Peach Pink Fabric (Color B)

Cut (2) 1" x 44" strips. Subcut (56) 1" squares.

Cut (2) 3/4" x 44" strips. Subcut (56) 3/4" squares.

Green Fabric (Color C)

Cut (1) 1" x 44" strip. Subcut (30) 1" squares.

Cut (1) 3/4" x 44" strip. Subcut (30) 3/4" squares.

Dark Plum Fabric (Color D)

Cut (1) 1" x 44" strip. Subcut (42) 1" squares.

Cut (1) 3/4" x 44" strip. Subcut (42) 3/4" squares.

Royal Blue Fabric (Color E)
Cut (1) 1" x 44" strip. Subcut (26) 1" squares.
Cut (1) 3/4" x 44" strip. Subcut (26) 3/4" squares.
Bright Pink Fabric (Color F)
Cut (1) 1" x 44" strip. Subcut (20) 1" squares.
Cut (1) 3/4" x 44" strip. Subcut (20) 3/4" squares.

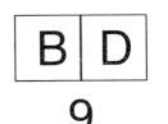

9

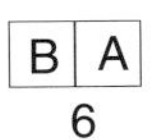

6

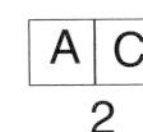

2

2

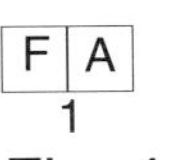

1

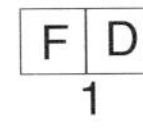

1

Fig. 4

PIECING INSTRUCTIONS

1. Make (55) Four Patch units (Fig. 1). The letters are the colors of the 1" squares. Make the number of units given under each Four Patch diagram. Chain-piece all the Two Patches for a single Four Patch unit at one time. Example: for the first Four Patch unit, chain-piece seven A/B Two Patches and seven C/A Two Patches in succession. Clip the Two Patch units apart. Press seams of the top A/B units to the left and of the bottom C/A units to the right. Trim seams (Fig. 2). Chain-piece the Two Patch units into Four Patch units. Trim seams (Fig. 3)
2. Make (21) Two Patch units (Fig. 4).
3. Using the photograph of the quilt as your guide, lay out all the Four Patch units, Two Patch units, 1 1/2" ecru squares, 1" x 1 1/2" rectangles and four 1" squares in the correct sequence on a flat surface. It is helpful to have a stabilizer underneath the units, such as a piece of flannel, felt or terry cloth.
4. Make (55) 1 1/2" square units with four connector corners (Fig. 5). On each corner of a 1 1/2" ecru square, color match a 3/4" square to the two squares of the Four Patch units it will meet (Fig. 6). Sew these 3/4" squares to the corners of the 1 1/2" squares with diagonal seams. You can draw diagonal lines on the back of the 3/4" squares or simply eyeball the diagonal seamline (Fig. 7).

HINT: It is helpful to place a dab of glue stick in each corner of an ecru square to hold the small squares securely. Press the squares over their seamlines toward the corners. Only trim back the seam allowance of the middle layer of fabric.

5. Make (21) 1" x 1 1/2" rectangle units with two connector corners (Fig. 8).
6. Make (2) 1" square units with one connector corner (Fig. 9).

Fig. 5

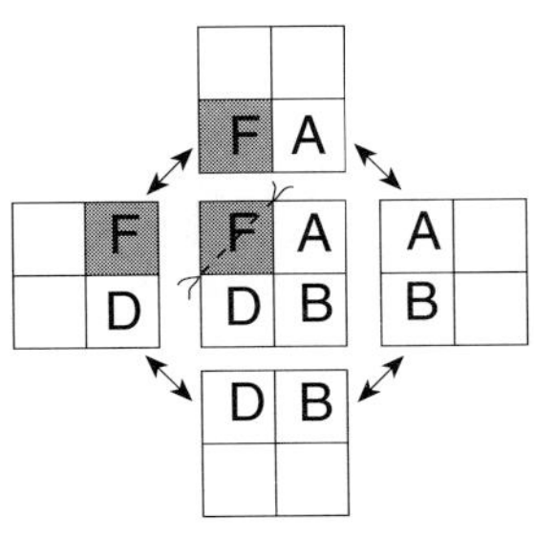

Fig. 6

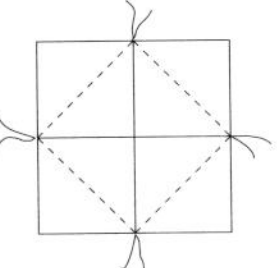
Fig. 7

ASSEMBLY

1. Sew the units into rows according to the layout. Press seams toward Two Patch and Four Patch units. Correct any errors in the pattern layout before trimming the seams.
2. Sew the rows together. Press seams downward. Trim seams if needed.
3. First Border: Cut (2) 1 1/8" x 44" strips of black. Subcut to fit and stitch to the quilt using the straight-cut corner method. Press the seams toward the outside of the quilt. Do not trim the seams.
4. Second Border: Cut (2) 2" x 44" strips of ecru. Subcut to fit and stitch to the quilt using the straight-cut corner method. Press the seams toward the outside of the quilt. Do not trim the seams.
5. Layer the quilt with thin batting and ecru backing.
6. Quilt as desired.
7 Finish the quilt with black binding.

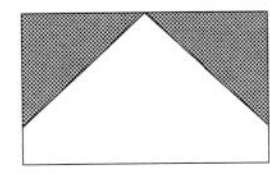
Fig. 8

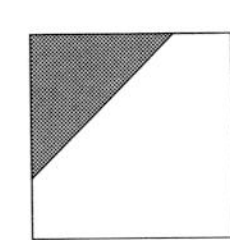
Fig. 9

CRAZY ANN

quilt shown on page 29

10 5/8" x 13"
12 Pieced Blocks

The traditional Crazy Ann block is a pinwheel variation formed by careful placement of flying geese units. Cutting and piecing oversized flying geese units and trimming them down to perfect sized units will make my tiny version go together quite easily. The original quilt was made of 20 pieced blocks and measured 78" x 86". It was completed in March 1915, in Topeka, La Grange County, Indiana. It is now in the collection of Rebecca Haarer.

Use 1/4" seam allowance; trim to 1/8" where needed to eliminate bulk.

1 1/2" Finished Blocks
Block A
Black and Dark Pink
Make (4)

FABRIC REQUIREMENTS
1 yard black for background, second border, binding and backing
1/4 yard dark pink
1/4 yard gold

CUTTING INSTRUCTIONS FOR BLOCKS
1. Dark pink fabric
Cut (5) 1 1/4" x 44" strips. Subcut (48) 1 1/4" x 1 3/4" rectangles and (96) 1 1/4" squares from the strips.
2. Black fabric
Cut (2) 1 1/4" x 44" strips. Subcut (16) 1 1/4" x 1 3/4" rectangles and (32) 1 1/4" squares from the strips.
3. Gold fabric
Cut (4) 1 1/4" x 44" strips. Subcut (32) 1 1/4" x 1 3/4" rectangles and (64) 1 1/4" squares from the strips.

1 1/2" Finished Blocks
Block B
Dark Pink and Gold
Make (8)

PIECING INSTRUCTIONS FOR BLOCKS
1. Make (16) Flying Geese units with pink for the center triangles and black for the background triangles (Fig. 1). Stitch a black square on the diagonal to one end of a pink rectangle. Press the square over the seamline to its corner. Trim the two lower layers (the seam allowance) to 1/8". Sew another black square to the other end of the rectangle. Press and trim as before.
HINT: Chain-piece the sewing of the squares to the same side of the rectangles in one step.

These units are oversized. Trim to 7/8" x 1 1/4". Using a 4" square ruler, trim the top of the unit to an exact 1/4" seam allowance (Fig. 2). Rotate the unit 180° so the triangle is pointing downward. Place 5/8" line from right edge of square ruler on the seam intersection of the unit and 7/8" line from top edge of square ruler on the trimmed seam allowance of the unit. Cut the next two sides of the unit (Fig. 3). Rotate the unit again so the triangle is now pointing upward. Place 1 1/4" line from right edge of square ruler on the left cut edge of unit and 7/8" line from top edge of square ruler on the bottom cut edge of unit. Trim the fourth side of unit (Fig. 4).

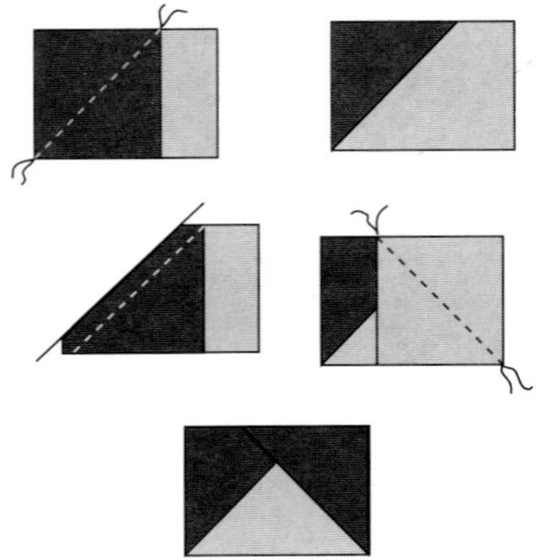

Fig. 1

2. Make (16) Flying Geese units with a black center triangle and pink as the background.
3. Make (32) Flying Geese units with a pink center triangle and gold as the background.
4. Make (32) Flying Geese units with a gold center triangle and pink as the background.
5. Sew all the above trimmed units into pairs. Press the seams in the direction of the arrows (Fig. 5 and Fig. 6).
6. Assemble (4) Block A's and (8) Block B's.

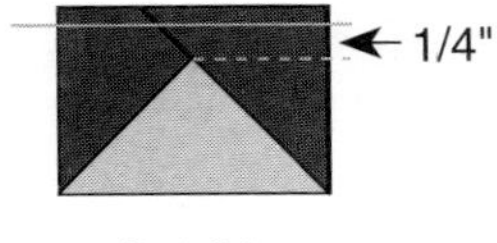

Cut #1
Fig. 2

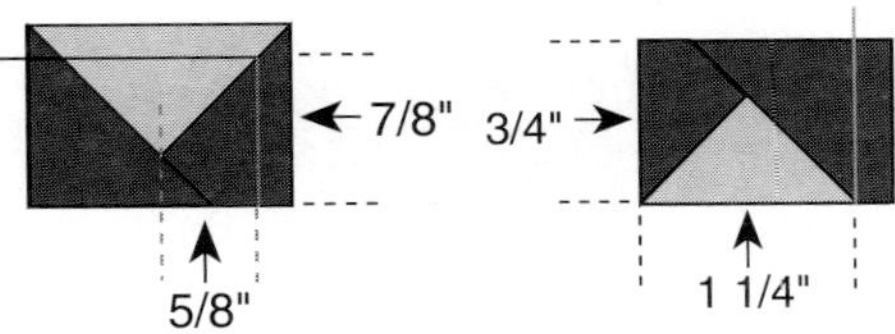

Cuts #2 and #3
Fig. 3

Cut #4
Fig. 4

ASSEMBLY

1. Cut (6) 2" squares of black for alternate blocks.
2. Cut (3) 3 1/2" squares of black and cut both ways diagonally to make (10) setting triangles.
3. Cut (2) 3 1/4" squares of black and cut diagonally in half to make (4) corner triangles.
4. Lay out all the units in correct sequence. Sew the units into diagonal rows, and press the seams away from the pieced blocks. Sew the rows together. Add the corners last. Trim the setting and corner triangles evenly around the assembled quilt top, leaving a 1/4" seam allowance.
5. First Border: Cut (1) 1 1/4" x 44" strip of pink. Cut (4) 1 1/4" squares of gold. Subcut (2) pink strips to fit the sides of the quilt top and sew to the quilt. Press the seams to the outside. Measure the width of the quilt top minus the side borders and add 1/2" to this measurement for seam allowances. Subcut (2) pink strips of this length and sew a gold square to each end of these strips. Press the seams toward the pink fabric. Stitch these border units to the top and bottom of the quilt top. Press the seams toward the outside of the quilt.
6. Second Border: Cut (1) 1 3/4" x 44" strip of black. Subcut to fit and stitch to the quilt using the straight-cut corner method. Press the seams toward the outside of the quilt.
7. Layer the quilt with thin batting and black backing.
8. Quilt as desired.
9. Finish the quilt with black binding.

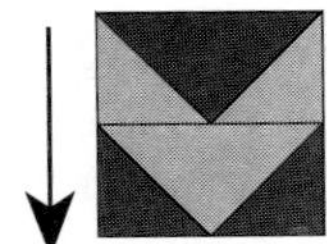

Fig. 5
Black and Dark Pink
Make (16)

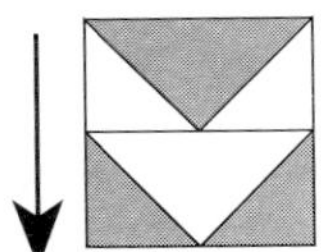

Fig. 6
Dark Pink and Gold
Make (32)

FAN

quilt shown on page 31

10" x 12"
12 Blocks

Victorian quilts had their influence even on Amish ladies, particularly in the Midwest. Many Fan quilts and Crazy quilts were made and embroidered by the Amish, who do not adorn themselves with external beauty. My tiny quilt resembles one made in 1927 in Elkhart County, Indiana. That original 76" x 85" quilt, containing 30 blocks with fans having nine blades, is in the collection of Diana Leone. Because my version has 2" blocks, I used only six blades in each fan to keep the proportions similar to the original quilt.

Use 1/4" seam allowance; trim to 1/8" where needed to eliminate bulk.

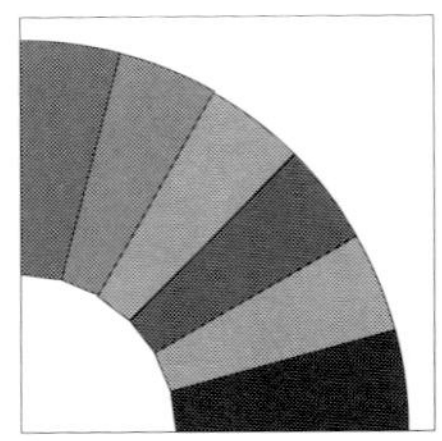

2" Finished Blocks

FABRIC REQUIREMENTS

1/2 yard black for background, second border and backing
1/8 yard bright red for fan blades and first border
1/4 yard gray for fan blades and binding
2 1/4" x 7" strip of each additional color for fan blades: dark red, bright pink, royal blue, light blue, purple, light purple, violet, medium violet, light violet, pink violet—Choose (12) different fabrics. I used colors which were similar to some of those in the original.

TEMPLATES

Trace patterns (A) and (B) onto template plastic. Cut out templates on the inside of the tracing lines. These templates include the seam allowance.

CUTTING

1. Cut a 2 1/4" x 7" strip of (12) fan blade colors.
2. Trace around Template (A) six times on four light fabric strips (Fig. 1). Place two unmarked fabric strips under each marked strip. Cut out (3) fan blades at one time, making a total of (72) fan blades. You may use a rotary cutter or a sharp pair of scissors.
3. Cut (1) 1 1/2" x 18" strip of black and subcut (12) 1 1/2" squares. Set Template (B) into the lower corner of a black square and trace the curve. Repeat for (3) more squares. Place a marked square on top of two unmarked squares and cut out (3) fan handles at one time. Repeat with the other squares.
4. Cut (1) 2 1/2" x 44" strip of black and subcut (12) 2 1/2" background squares.

Fig. 1

PIECING

Randomly piece fan blades into (12) sets of six. Press seams in one direction. Trim seams to 1/8".

APPLIQUÉ

1. Appliqué the top curve of the fan to the 2 1/2" squares, turning under the 1/4" seam allowance.
2. Appliqué the top curve of the fan handle to the lower part of the fan blades, turning under the 1/4" seam allowance. Make sure the handles end up square with the 2 1/2" background squares. Cut away the excess background square almost up to the seam allowance at the top of each fan to eliminate bulk.

ASSEMBLY OF BLOCKS

1. Sew the fan blocks into rows according to the photo. Press the seams of each row in alternate directions.
2. Sew the rows together.

EMBROIDERY

I used two strands of a gold embroidery thread and worked the Herringbone Stitch at the top of the fan blades on the black background and at the top of the blade handles. The stitch is worked from left to right (Fig. 2). An option would be to use a fancy sewing machine stitch.

ASSEMBLY

1. First Border: Cut (1) 1" x 44" strip of bright red. Subcut to fit and sew to the quilt using the straight-cut corner method. Press the seams toward the outside of the quilt.
2. Second Border: Cut (1) 2" x 44" strip of black. Subcut to fit and sew to the quilt using the straight-cut corner method. Press the seams toward the outside of the quilt.
3. Layer the quilt with thin batting and black backing.
4. Quilt as desired.
5. Finish the quilt with gray binding.

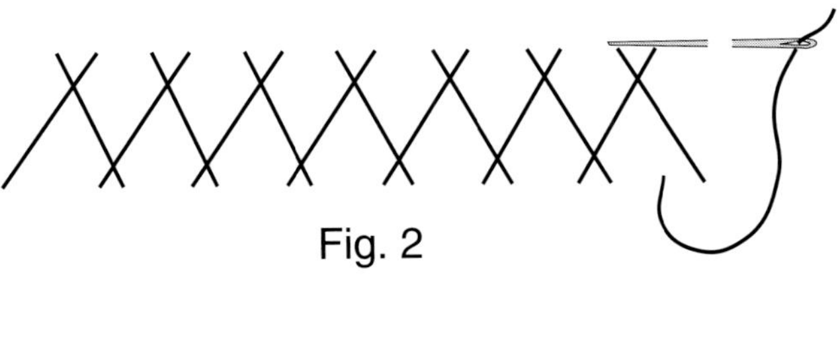

Fig. 2

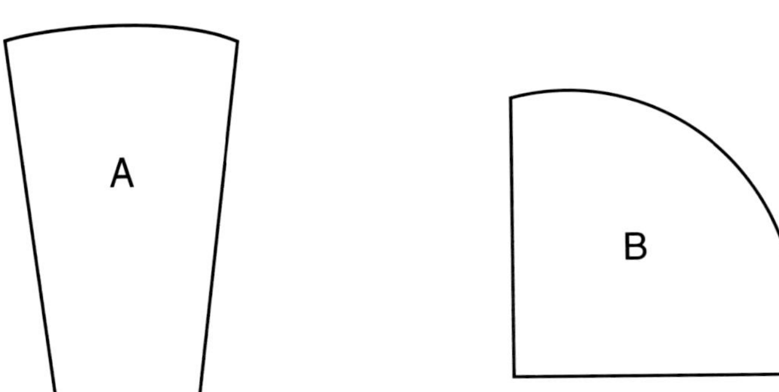

JACOB'S LADDER

quilt shown on page 36

14 1/2" x 19"
24 Blocks

Genesis 28:12 says of Jacob, "And he had a dream, and behold, a ladder was set on the earth with its top reaching to heaven..." No doubt, the Biblical name of this traditional block made this pattern appeal to the Amish women. The original quilt was made in La Grange County, Indiana, in 1920. It is 68" x 80" and contains 48 blocks. Rebecca Haarer, who now owns it, says that originally the background fabric was also a blue but now only the one block has retained its blue color.

Use 1/4" seam allowance; trim to 1/8" where needed to eliminate bulk.

2 1/4" Finished Blocks

FABRIC REQUIREMENTS

1 3/8 yards black for blocks, second border, backing and binding
5/8 yard off-white for background (You may use several off-white fabrics.)
1/8 yard medium blue for one block and first border

CUTTING AND PIECING OF UNITS

1. Make (115) Four Patch units of black and off-white (Fig. 1). Cut (6) 1 1/8" x 44" strips of black and (6) 1 1/8" x 44" strips of off-white. Sew (6) sets of these two colors together lengthwise (Fig. 2).
HINT: Sewing these strips together with 1/8" seams eliminates having to trim them to 1/8". Press seams toward the black. Subcut (230) 1 1/8" wide segments from the above set-ups. Trim seams to 1/8" if you sewed strips together with 1/4" seams (Fig. 3). Chain-piece these segments into (115) Four Patch units (Fig. 4). Clip units apart and press seams to one side. Trim seams. Trim each Four Patch to a 1 1/4" unit with a square ruler. Align the 5/8" lines of the square ruler on the upper right black square of the unit. Cut the right and top sides. Rotate the unit 180° and align the 1 1/4" lines on the two cut edges; cut the remaining two sides of the unit (Fig. 5).
2. Make (5) Four Patch units from black and blue (Fig. 6). Cut (1) 1 1/8" x 13" strip of black and (1) 1 1/8" x 13" strip of blue. Sew the (2) strips together lengthwise. Subcut (10) 1 1/8" wide segments. Chain-piece these segments into (5) Four Patch units and trim each unit to 1 1/4" squares.

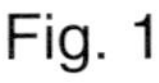

Fig. 1

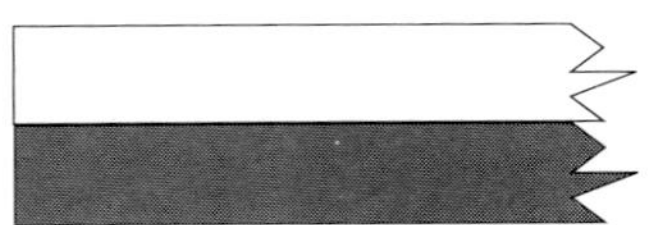

Fig. 2

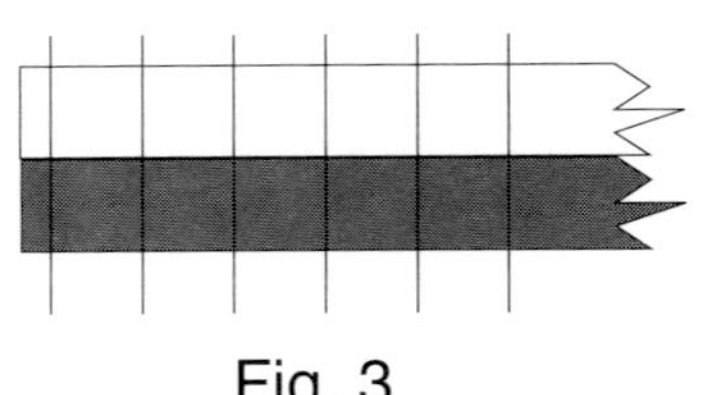

Fig. 3

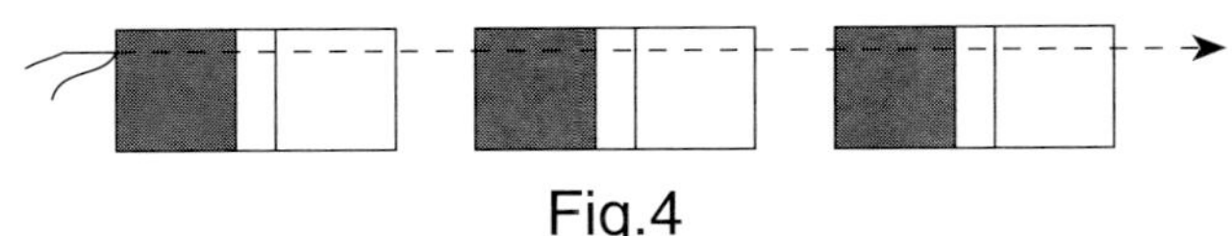

Fig.4

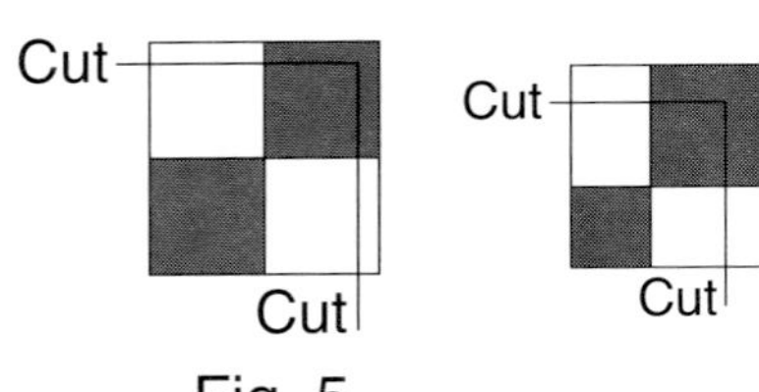

Fig. 5

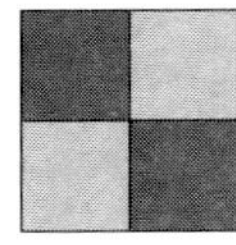

Fig. 6

3. Make (92) 1 1/4" half-square triangle units of a black and off-white combination and (4) of a black and blue combination (Fig. 7). Cut (2 1/2) 2" x 44" strips of black; (2 1/2) 2" x 44" strips of off-white; and (1) 2" x 4" strip of blue. Subcut (48) 2" squares of black, (46) 2" squares of off-white and (2) 2" squares of medium blue.

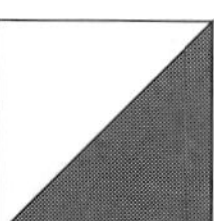

Fig. 7

Using a fine-line pencil, draw a diagonal line on the back of all the off-white and blue squares. With right sides together place a light square on top of a black square and sew a 1/4" seam on one side of the marked diagonal line.

HINT: Sewing these seams with a 1/8" seam will eliminate having to trim them back. Continue chain-piecing the seams of the remaining (47) units. Chain-piece 1/4" or 1/8" seams on the other side of the diagonal lines of all (48) units. Clip the units apart (Fig. 8).

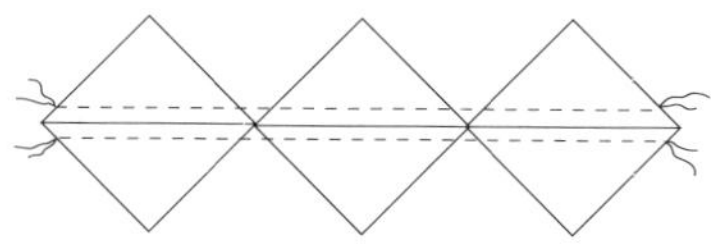

Fig. 8

Cut each unit in half on its diagonal line. Press seams toward the dark fabric. Trim each square to 1 1/4" with a square ruler. Align the diagonal line of the square ruler on the unit's bias seam and cut the top two edges. Rotate the half-square triangle unit 180° and position the 1 1/4" lines of the square ruler on the first two cut edges. Make the last two cuts (Fig. 9). Trim the seams to 1/8" if 1/4" seams were used.

4. Assemble the blocks. In order to make as many seams butt each other as possible, sew the units into two different block arrangements. The seams of the two blocks will be pressed in opposite directions. Block A—Make (12) blocks from black and off-white units (Fig. 10). Sew the units into rows. Press the seams toward the Four Patches. Sew the rows together. Press the seams toward the center.

Block B—Make (11) blocks from black and off-white units and (1) block from black and blue units (Fig. 11). Sew the units into rows. Press the seams toward the half-square triangle units. Sew the rows together. Press the seams away from the center. Sew the blocks into rows as illustrated below (Fig. 12).

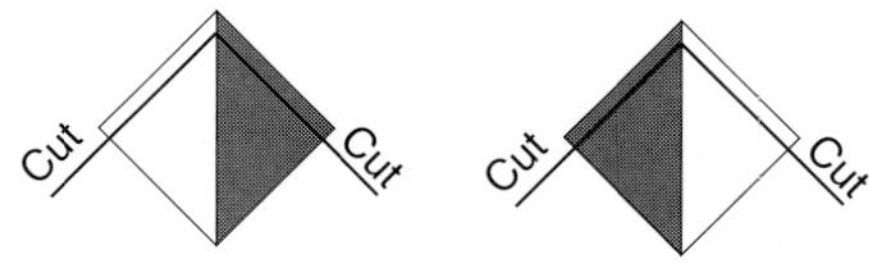

Fig. 9

HINT: Where two seams will not butt each other, it is helpful to put a dab of glue stick on one seam allowance and stick the other to it. Press the seams toward the Block A's. Sew the rows together.

ASSEMBLY

1. First Border: Cut (2) 1 1/4" x 44" strips of blue. Subcut to fit and stitch to the quilt using the straight-cut corner method. Press the seams toward the outside of the quilt.
2. Second border: Cut (2) 2 1/2" x 44" strips of black. Subcut to fit and stitch to the quilt. Press the seams toward the outside of the quilt.
3. Layer the quilt with thin batting and black backing.
4. Quilt as desired.
5. Finish the quilt with black binding.

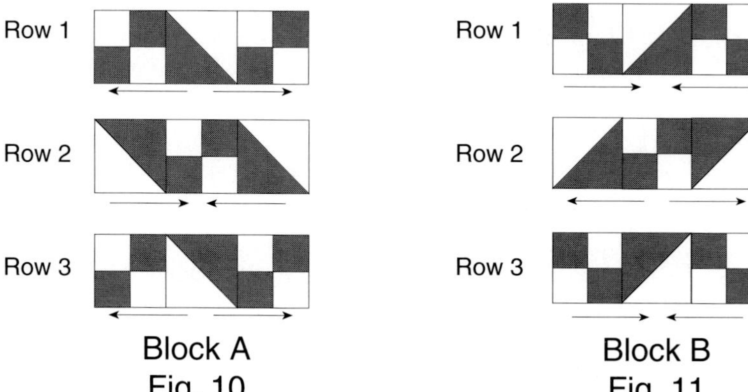

Block A
Fig. 10

Block B
Fig. 11

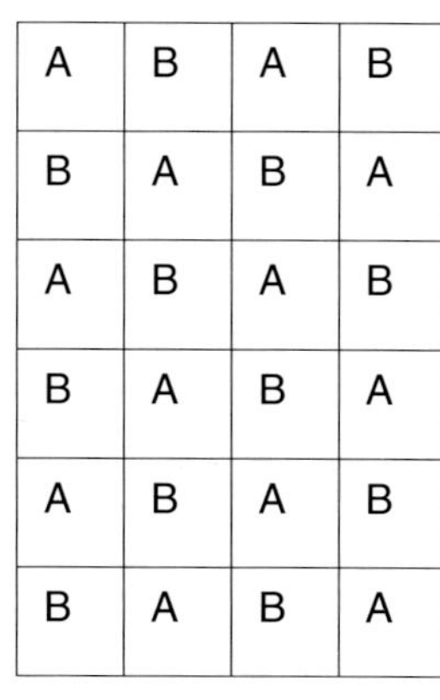

A	B	A	B
B	A	B	A
A	B	A	B
B	A	B	A
A	B	A	B
B	A	B	A

Fig. 12

AMISH BASKETS

quilt shown on page 34

11" x 13"
6 Pieced Blocks

Most Amish Basket quilts come from the Midwest. The quilt which inspired this miniature was shown on a Georgia Bonesteel television program about Amish quilts. Georgia interviewed Rebecca Haarer, a collector of Amish quilts, who lives in Shipshewana, Indiana. She showed a crib-size basket quilt in these colors, which was made in Indiana in the early 1900s.

Use 1/4" seam allowance; trim to 1/8" where needed to eliminate bulk.

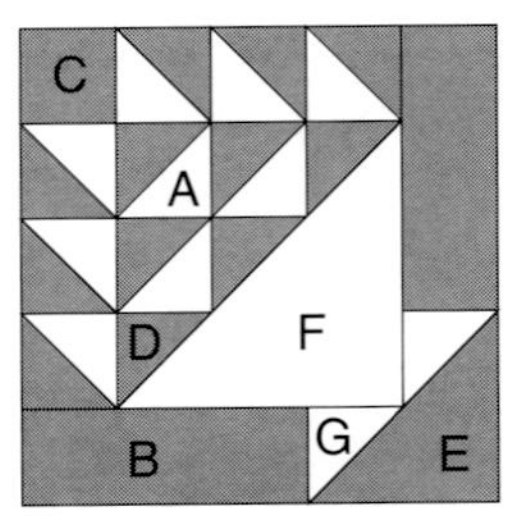

1 7/8" Finished Blocks

FABRIC REQUIREMENTS
1/2 yard medium blue for background, second border and backing
1/4 yard white for baskets, first border and binding

CUTTING (Letters correspond to the block diagram.)
A. From each fabric, cut (1) 1 3/4' x 44" strip and (1) 1 3/4" x 6" strip. Subcut strips into (27) 1 3/4" squares of each color.
B. Cut (1) 7/8" x 21" strip of blue and subcut (12) 7/8" x 1 5/8" segments.
C. Cut (1) 7/8" x 6" strip of blue and subcut (6) 7/8" squares.
D. Cut (1) 1 1/4" x 12" strip of blue and subcut (9) 1 1/4" squares. Cut squares diagonally in half to make (18) triangles.
E. Cut (3) 2" squares of blue and cut diagonally in half to make (6) triangles.
F. Cut (3) 2 1/2" squares of white and cut diagonally in half to make (6) triangles.
G. Cut (1) 1 1/4" x 8" strip of white and subcut (6) 1 1/4" squares. Cut squares diagonally in half to make (12) triangles.

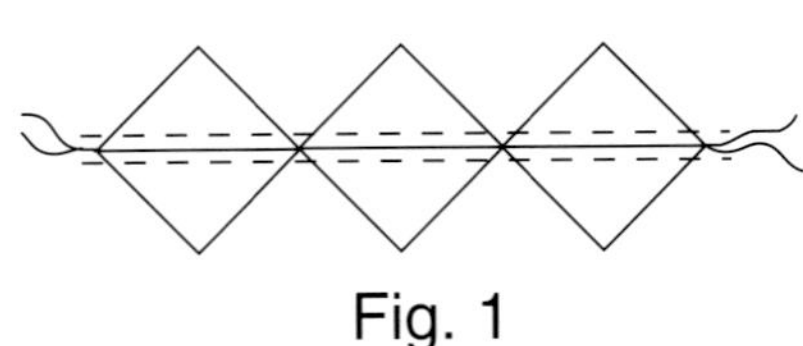

Fig. 1

HALF-SQUARE TRIANGLE UNITS
Make (54) 7/8" units of blue and white, as follows.
1. Draw a diagonal line on the back of the (27) white squares. With right sides together, place a marked white square on top of a blue square and sew a 1/4" seam on one side of the marked diagonal line. HINT: Sewing these seams with a 1/8" seam will eliminate having to trim them back. Continue chain-piecing the seams of the remaining (26) units. Chain-piece 1/4" or 1/8" seams on the other side of the diagonal lines of all (27) units. Clip units apart (Fig. 1).
2. Cut each unit in half on its diagonal line. Press seams toward the blue fabric.
3. Trim each square to 7/8" with a square ruler. Align the diagonal line of the square ruler on the unit's bias seam and cut the top two edges. Rotate the half-square triangle unit 180° and position the 7/8" lines of the square ruler on the first two cut edges. Make the last two cuts (Fig. 2). Trim the seams to 1/8" if 1/4" seams were used.

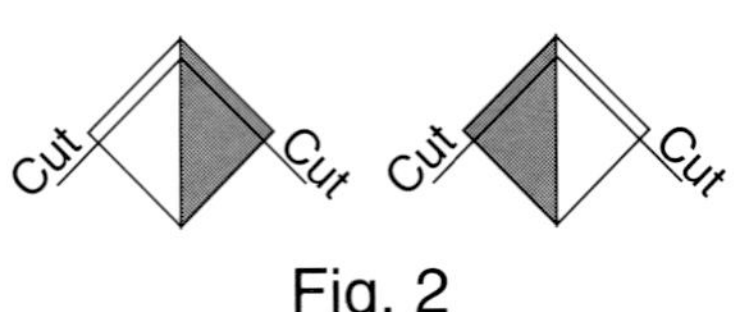

Fig. 2

PIECING (For each basket, repeat steps 1-5.)

1. Sew 7/8" half-square triangle units and small blue triangles into rows as illustrated. Press the seams in the direction of the arrows and trim. Sew the rows together. Press the seams downward and trim (Fig. 3).
2. Sew an oversized white basket triangle to the above unit. Press the seam toward the white triangle (Fig. 4). Trim the sides of the triangle even with the pieced triangle.
3. Make two basket handle units. Press the seams in the direction of the arrows and trim. Sew these units to the basket section. Press the seams in the direction of the arrows and trim (Fig. 5).

Fig. 3

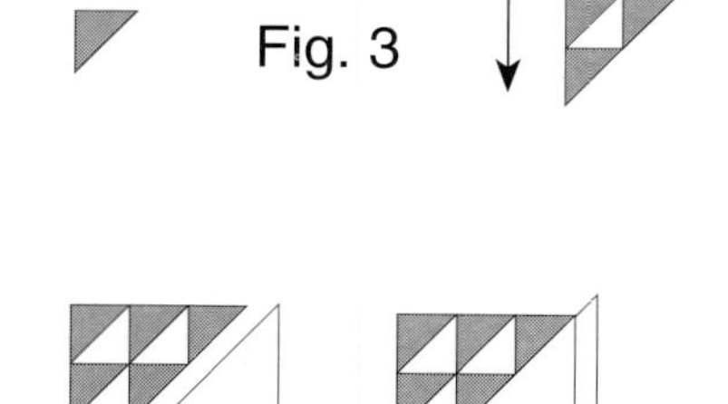

Fig. 4

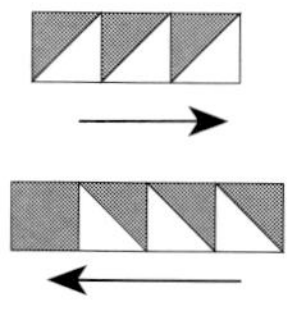

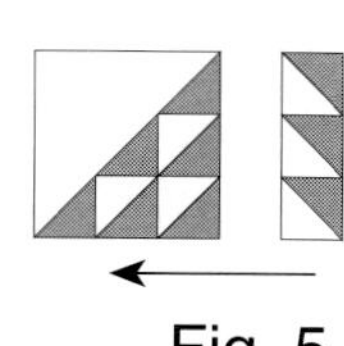

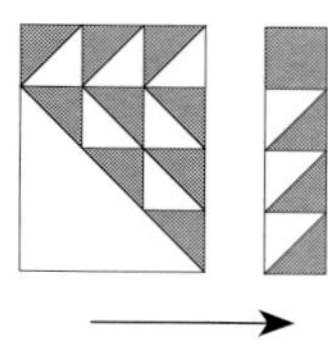

Fig. 5

4. Sew the small white triangles to the blue background rectangles. Press the seams toward the rectangles. Sew these two units to the sides of the square basket section (Fig. 6). Press the seams toward the rectangle units and trim.
5. Sew an oversized blue triangle to the bottom of the basket section. Press seam toward the blue triangle. Trim the sides of the triangle even with the basket section (Fig. 7).

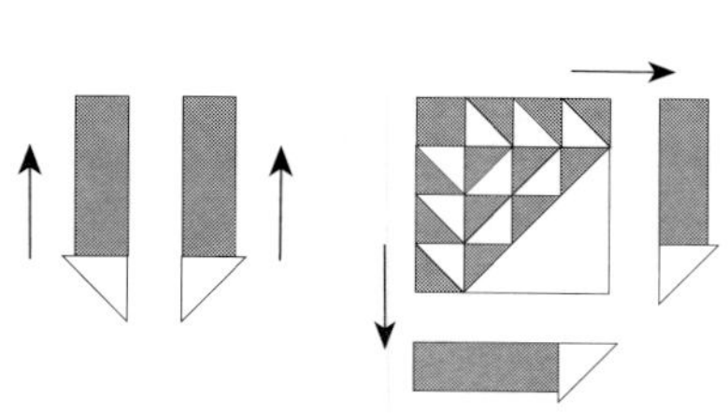

Fig. 6

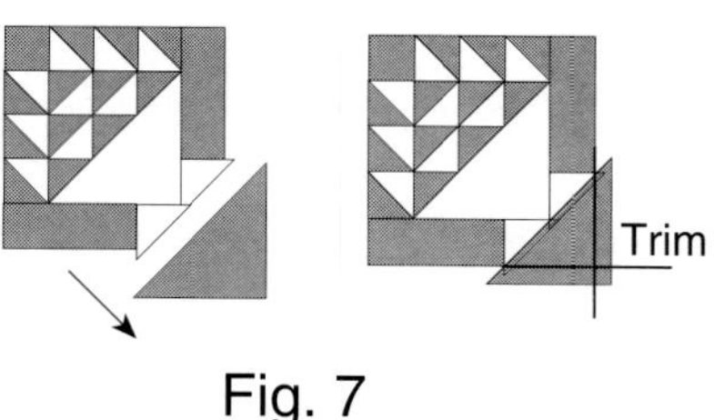

Fig. 7

ASSEMBLY

1. Cut (2) 2 3/8" squares of blue for alternate blocks.
2. Cut (2) 4 1/2" squares of blue and cut diagonally both ways to make (6) setting triangles.
3. Cut (2) 4 1/4" squares of blue and cut diagonally in half to make (4) corner triangles.
4. Lay out all the units in sequence according to the photo of the quilt. Sew the units into diagonal rows. Press the seams away from the pieced blocks. Sew the rows together. Add the corners last. Trim the setting and corner triangles evenly around the assembled quilt top, leaving approximately 3/4" beyond the corners of the blocks. This will float the basket blocks.
5. First Border: Cut (1) 1 1/4" x 44" strip of white. Subcut to fit and stitch to the quilt using the straight-cut corner method. Press the seams toward the outside of the quilt.
6. Second Border: Cut (2) 2" x 44" strips of blue. Subcut to fit and stitch to the quilt using the straight-cut corner method. Press the seams toward the outside of the quilt.
7. Layer the quilt with thin batting and blue backing.
8. Quilt as desired.
9. Finish the quilt with white binding.

RAIL FENCE

quilt shown on page 29

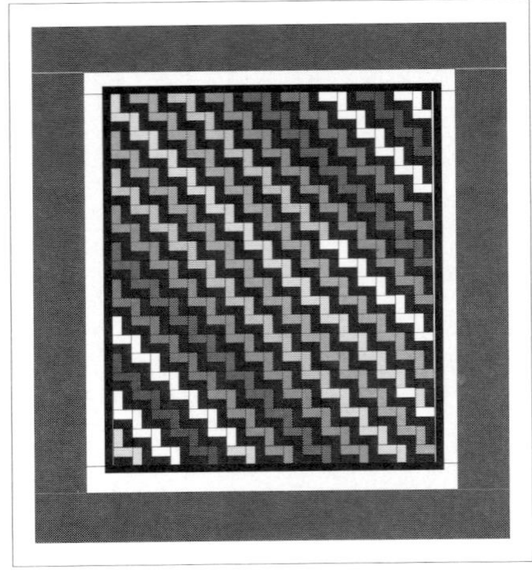

12" x 13"

The traditional Rail Fence or Streak of Lightning pattern is very easy for us to cut and piece because of the rotary cutter and strip methods. However, in 1930 an Amish lady had to cut 680 separate rectangles to make the original 76" x 84" quilt in Loudenville, Ohio. Judi Boisson Antique American Quilts, New York, owns that Amish masterpiece. You can make this tiny version containing all 680 pieces by choosing 13 similar colors and paying careful attention to the color placement of the units. Notice that several of the lightning streaks contain pieces of more than one color.

Use 1/4" seam allowance; trim to 1/8" where needed to eliminate bulk.

1/2"
Finished Units

FABRIC REQUIREMENTS

3/4 yard black for strips, first and third borders and backing
1/4 yard white for strips, second border and binding
1/8 yard of each of the following: cream, light blue, medium blue, dark blue, violet, rust, medium pink, dark pink, dark teal, turquoise and dark brown

CUT THE FOLLOWING STRIPS FOR RAIL UNITS

(9) 3/4" x 44" strips of black
(1) 3/4" x 27" strip of cream
(1) 3/4" x 11" strip of white
(1) 3/4" x 38" strip of light blue
(1) 3/4" x 20" strip of medium blue
(1) 3/4" x 9" strip of dark blue
(1) 3/4" x 16" strip of violet
(1) 3/4" x 33" strip of rust
(1) 3/4" x 44" strip plus 17" of medium pink
(1) 3/4" x 44" strip plus 9" of dark pink
(1) 3/4" x 19" strip of dark teal
(1) 3/4" x 44" strip plus 24" of turquoise
(1) 3/4" x 3" strip of dark brown

PIECING OF RAIL UNITS (340 units needed)

1. Subcut the black fabric strips into lengths to fit each of the other strips you cut. Sew a corresponding black strip lengthwise to each of these other strips. These can all be chain-pieced in succession. Press all the seams toward the black fabric. Trim the seams of each strip set-up.
2. Subcut the following 1" segments from each strip set-up. It is helpful to keep each of the color units in separate piles.

(26) Cream
(10) White
(37) Light Blue

(19) Medium Blue
(8) Dark Blue
(15) Violet
(32) Rust
(58) Medium Pink
(50) Dark Pink
(18) Dark Teal
(65) Turquoise
(2) Dark Brown

3. Following the photograph of the quilt, sew the corresponding units into rows. There are 17 units in each of 20 rows. Press the seams of each row toward the vertical units. Trim the seams.

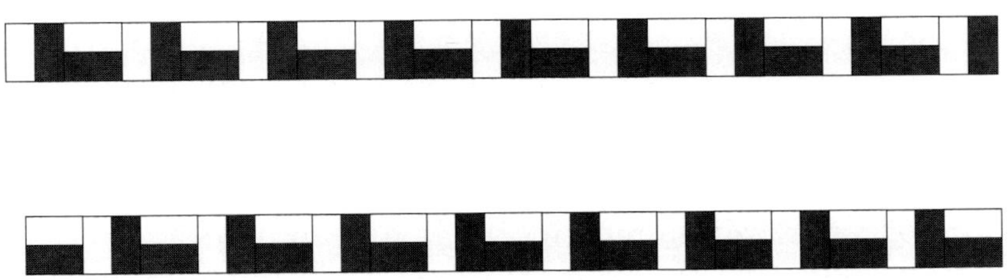

4. Lay out each row in proper sequence on a piece of flannel, felt or terry cloth and check the design for proper color placement. Correct any errors at this time.
5. Sew the rows together. Press the seams downward and trim.

ASSEMBLY

1. First Border: Cut (1) 1" x 44" strip of black. Subcut to fit and stitch to the quilt using the straight-cut corner method. Press the seams toward the outside of the quilt; trim to 1/8". Trim this first black border to exactly 1/2" from the seamline.
2. Second Border: Cut (1) 7/8" x 44" strip of white. Subcut to fit and stitch to the quilt using the straight-cut corner method. Press the seams toward the outside of the quilt. You do not need to trim these seams.
3. Third Border: Cut (2) 1 1/2" x 44" strips of black. Subcut to fit and stitch to the quilt using the straight-cut corner method. Press the seams toward the outside of the quilt.
4. Layer the quilt with thin batting and black backing.
5. Quilt as desired.
6. Finish the quilt with white binding.

CROWN OF THORNS

quilt shown on page 33

11" x 15"
6 Pieced Blocks

The name of this traditional block refers to when Christ was forced to wear a Crown of Thorns on the day of His crucifixion. Perhaps this is why the pattern would appeal to the Amish. The original 80" x 94" quilt, containing 20 pieced blocks, was made in Holmes County, Ohio, in 1930. It is in the collection of Catherine H. Anthony. Recently, I visited this county and saw many Amish ladies enjoying the fellowship of quilting together at large frames.

Use 1/4" seam allowance; trim to 1/8" where needed to eliminate bulk.

2 1/2"
Finished Blocks

FABRIC REQUIREMENTS
3/4 yard black for background, second border and backing
1/4 yard medium pink (blue-tone) for first border and binding
1/8 yard of each of the six following colors: bright red, bright blue, yellow, bright pink, olive green and rust

CUTTING FOR BLOCKS
Black Fabric for (6) Pieced Blocks:
1. Cut (2) 1 3/4" x 44" strips.
Subcut (36) 1 3/4" squares.
2. Cut (2) 1" x 44" strips.
Subcut (54) 1" squares.
Contrast Fabric for (1) Pieced Block:
1. Cut (1) 1 3/4" x 11" strip.
Subcut (6) 1 3/4" squares.
2. Cut (1) 1" x 7" strip.
Subcut (2) 1" x 2" segments and (2) 1" squares.

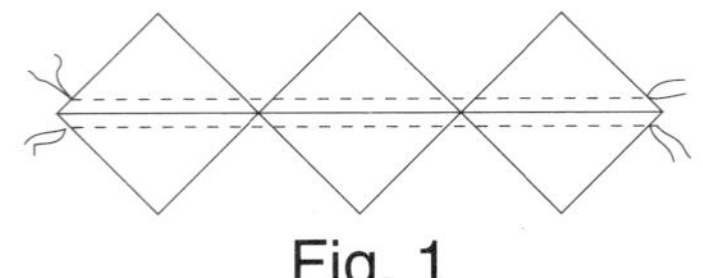

Fig. 1

PIECING FOR ONE BLOCK
1. Make (12) 1" half-square triangle units of a black and contrast combination. Draw a diagonal line on the back of (6) 1 3/4" squares of contrast fabric. With right sides together, place a marked square on top of a black square and sew a 1/4" seam on one side of the marked diagonal line. HINT: Sewing these seams with a 1/8" seam will eliminate having to trim them back. Continue chain-piecing the seams of the remaining (5) units. Chain-piece 1/4" or 1/8" seams on the other side of the diagonal lines on all (6) units (Fig. 1). Clip the units apart.

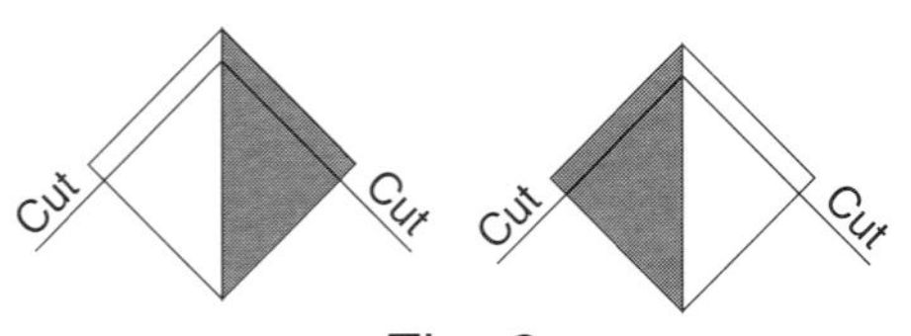

Fig. 2

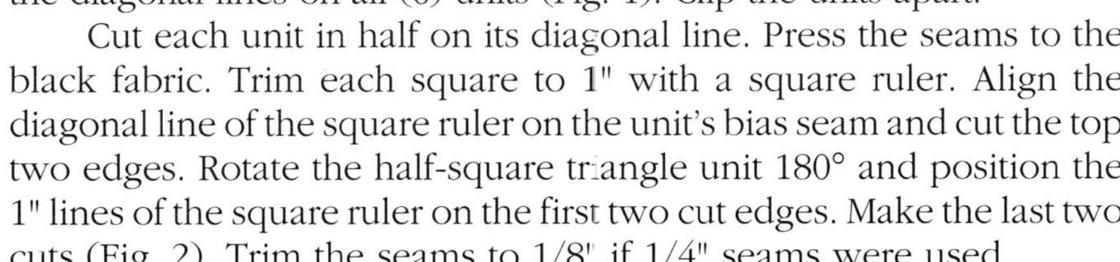

Cut each unit in half on its diagonal line. Press the seams to the black fabric. Trim each square to 1" with a square ruler. Align the diagonal line of the square ruler on the unit's bias seam and cut the top two edges. Rotate the half-square triangle unit 180° and position the 1" lines of the square ruler on the first two cut edges. Make the last two cuts (Fig. 2). Trim the seams to 1/8" if 1/4" seams were used.

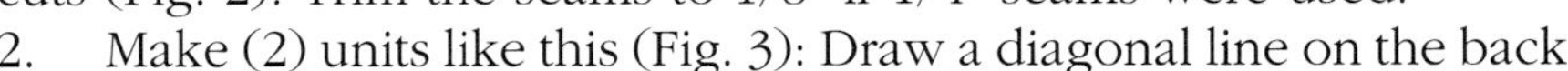

2. Make (2) units like this (Fig. 3): Draw a diagonal line on the back

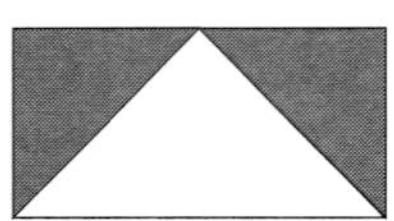

Fig. 3

of (4) 1" black squares, or press in diagonal creases. Sew squares on the diagonal to each end of the (2) 1" x 2" rectangles of contrast fabric (Fig. 4). Press the squares over their seamlines to the corners. Trim the two lower layers (the seam allowance) to 1/8".

3. Sew the units into rows as illustrated (Fig. 5). Press the seams in the direction of the arrows. Trim the seams where needed. Sew the rows together. Press the seams toward the center row. Trim the seams meeting at the center row.

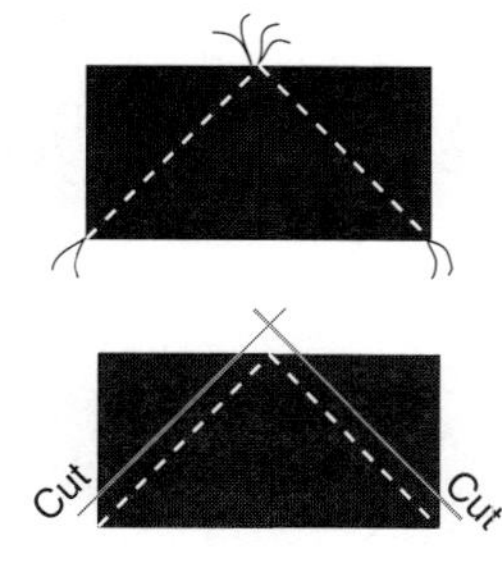

Fig. 4

ASSEMBLY

1. Cut (2) 3" squares of black for alternate blocks.
2. Cut (2) 5 1/4" squares of black and cut diagonally both ways to make (6) setting triangles.
3. Cut (2) 5" squares of black and cut in half diagonally to make (4) corner triangles.
4. Lay out all the units in correct sequence according to the photo of the quilt. Sew the units into diagonal rows. Press the seams away from the pieced blocks. Sew the rows together. Add the corners last. Trim the setting and corner triangles evenly around the assembled quilt top, leaving a 1/4" seam allowance.
5. First Border: Cut (1) 1" x 44" strip of medium pink. Subcut to fit and stitch to the quilt using the straight-cut corner method. Press the seams toward the outside of the quilt.
6. Second Border: Cut (2) 1 3/4" x 44" strips of black. Subcut to fit and stitch to the quilt using the straight-cut corner method. Press the seams toward the outside of the quilt.
7. Layer the quilt with thin batting and black backing.
8. Quilt as desired.
9. Finish the quilt with medium pink binding.

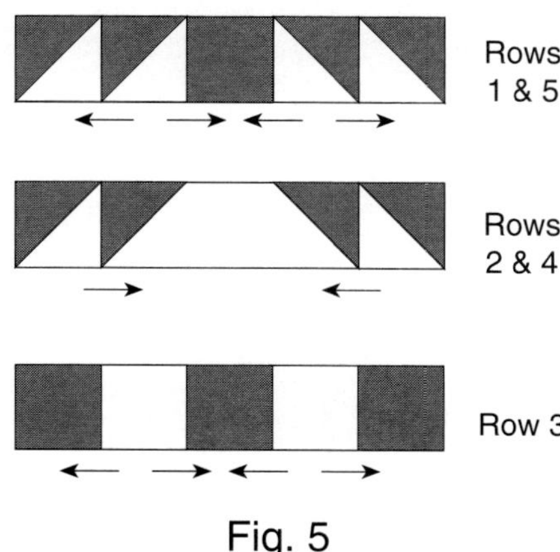

Fig. 5

PINWHEEL (VARIATION)

quilt shown on page 33

10 1/2" x 12 1/2"
12 Pieced Blocks

This traditional block has several other names, such as Waterwheel and Twin Sisters. The windmill, which provided power to the Amish homes and barns, probably inspired the Amish to use this block. The original 66" x 76" Amish quilt contained 30 pieced blocks. It was dated February 12, 1925, La Grange County, Indiana, and is owned by Rebecca Haarer. My tiny version is pieced very quickly by sewing bias strips together and cutting triangle units with a square ruler.

Use 1/4" seam allowance; trim to 1/8" where needed to eliminate bulk.

1 1/2"
Finished Blocks

FABRIC REQUIREMENTS

5/8 yard medium blue for background, second border and backing
1/4 yard black for (12) blocks
1/4 yard dark pink for (4) blocks and binding
1/4 yard yellow for (8) blocks
1/8 yard gray for first border

CUTTING AND PIECING

1. From the 1/4" yard of black fabric, cut (9) 1 1/4" wide bias strips. Lay a 45° angle line of a long ruler on the bottom edge of the fabric and make the first cut. Line up the 1 1/4" line of the ruler on this cut edge and cut the first strip. Cut (8) more 1 1/4" wide bias strips (Fig. 1).
2. From the 1/4 yard of yellow fabric, cut (6) 1 3/4" wide bias strips.
3. From the 1/4 yard of dark pink fabric, cut (3) 1 3/4" wide bias strips.
4. Sew a black strip to each of the other strips lengthwise. Press seams toward the black strips. Trim the seams to 1/8".
5. Subcut (32) 2" wide segments from the (6) black and yellow strip units and (16) 2" wide segments from the (3) black and dark pink strip units (Fig. 2).
6. With the 4" square ruler trim the black strip of each unit to an exact 11/16" from the seamline (Fig. 3).

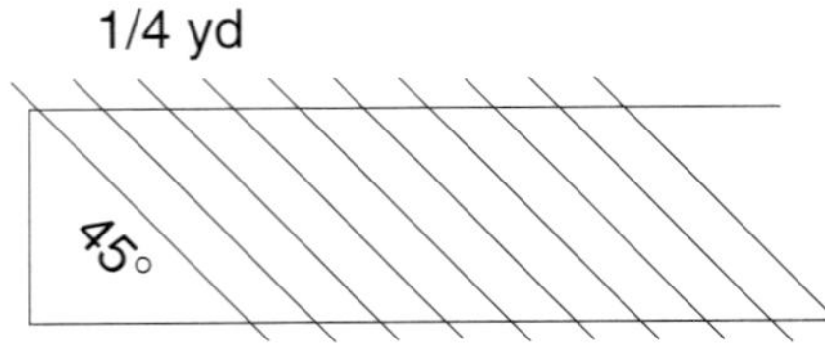

Fig. 1

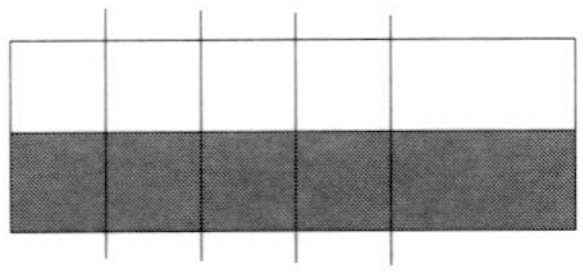

Fig. 2

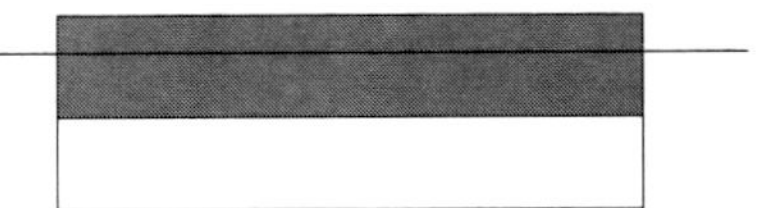

Fig. 3

7. Cut a triangle from each unit by lining up a 45° diagonal line of the square ruler on the left edge of the unit and the 2 3/4" marking on the side of the ruler on the bottom edge of the black fabric (Fig. 4).
8. Sew the triangle units into pairs of like color combinations. Make sure the triangles on the bottom are facing this way (Fig. 5). Press the seams toward the entire black strip. Trim the seams.
9. Sew two pairs of like color combinations together to form (8) black and yellow blocks and (4) black and dark pink blocks. These seams can be left at 1/4" and pressed open or trimmed to 1/8" and pressed to one side.

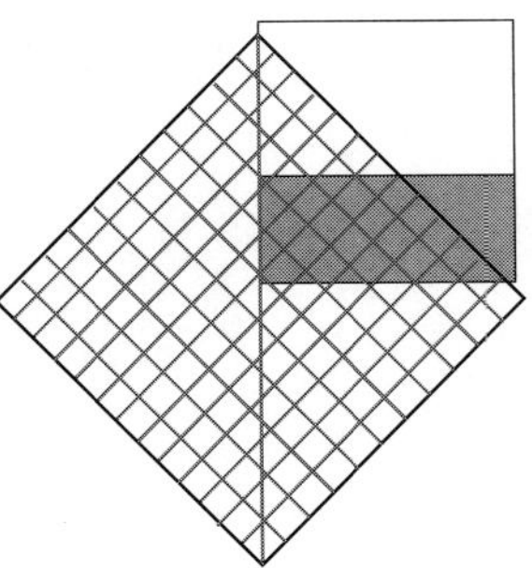

Fig. 4

ASSEMBLY

1. Cut (6) 2" squares of medium blue fabric for alternate blocks.
2. Cut (3) 3 1/2" squares of medium blue fabric and cut both ways diagonally to make (10) setting triangles.
3. Cut (2) 3 1/4" squares of medium blue and cut diagonally in half to make (4) corner triangles.
4. Lay out the units in sequence. Sew the units into diagonal rows, and press the seams away from the pieced blocks. Sew the rows together. Add the corners last. Trim the setting and corner triangles evenly around the assembled quilt top, leaving a 1/4" seam allowance.
5. First Border: Cut (1) 1" x 44" strip of gray. Subcut to fit and stitch to the quilt using the straight-cut corner method. Press the seams toward the outside of the quilt.
6. Second Border: Cut (1) 1 7/8" x 44" strip of medium blue. Subcut to fit and stitch to the quilt using the straight-cut corner method. Press the seams toward the outside of the quilt.
7. Layer the quilt with thin batting and medium blue backing.
8. Quilt as desired.
9. Finish the quilt with dark pink binding.

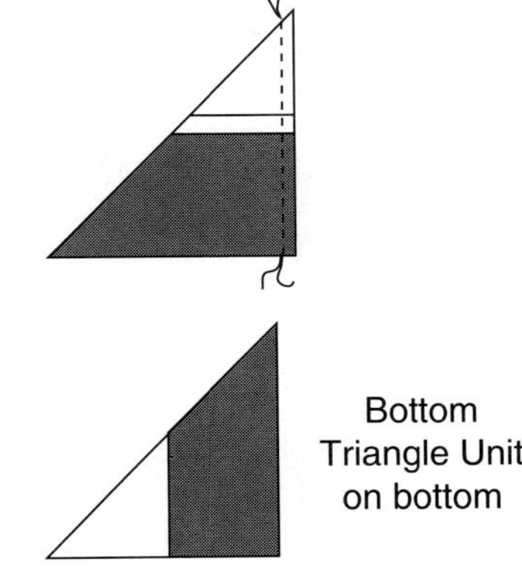

Fig. 5

TUMBLING BLOCKS

quilt shown on page 29

11" x 12 1/2"

The Tumbling Blocks design is usually done with set-in seams. I wanted to do an Amish miniature of the design for this collection, but in an easier way. One night in the wee hours, the method jumped at me from a picture of an antique Amish quilt. Rather than piecing the block sections in the customary horizontal rows, I could piece them in vertical rows by adding one seam to one piece of each block. The Amish quilt, which inspired this tiny quilt of 294 pieces, is 70" x 79" and was made in Southern Wisconsin in 1930-40. Cyndi Davis owns that antique blue quilt.

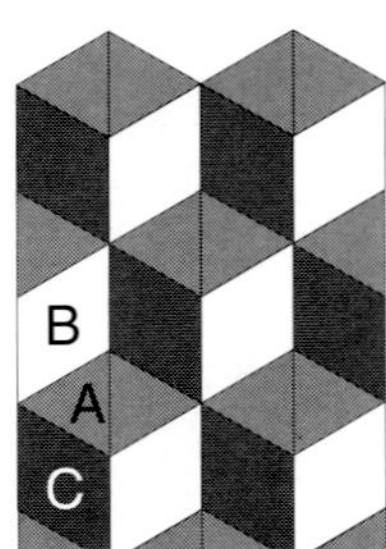

Use 1/4" seam allowance; trim to 1/8" where needed to eliminate bulk.

FABRIC REQUIREMENTS
3/4 yard medium blue for piecing, second border and backing
1/8 yard light blue for piecing and first border
1/4 yard navy blue for piecing and binding
NOTE: The letters in the Cutting and Piecing directions refer to the sections of the Tumbling Blocks.

CUTTING (A ruler marked with 60° angles is required.)
A. Medium Blue: Cut (154) 60° triangles.
Cut (4) 1 1/4" x 44" strips. Keep each strip folded in four layers. At the left end of a layered strip, align the 60° angle of the ruler with the top edge of the strip and cut, going toward the right at the top edge. Align the opposite 60° angle with the bottom of the strip and cut, meeting the top point of the first cut. Keep alternating the 60° angles of the ruler with the top and bottom edges of the strip to make the cuts (Fig. 1).

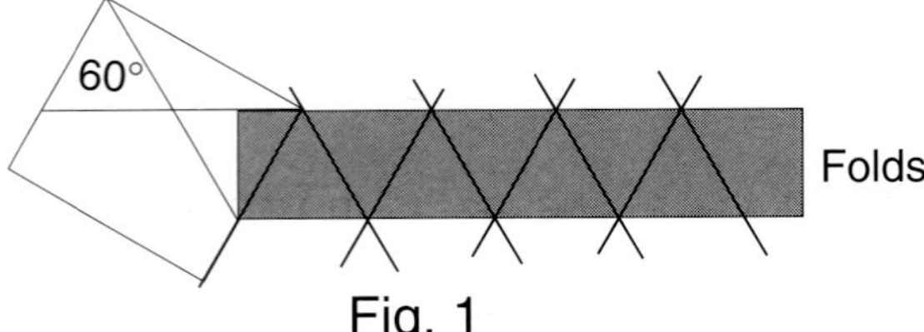

Fig. 1

B. Light Blue: Cut (70) 60° diamonds.
Cut (2) 1" x 44" strips. Keep each strip folded in four layers. At the left end of a layered strip, align the 60° angle with the bottom edge of the strip and cut. Make cuts parallel to the 60° angle every inch (Fig. 2).
C. Navy Blue: Cut (70) 60° diamonds from (2) 1" x 44" strips.

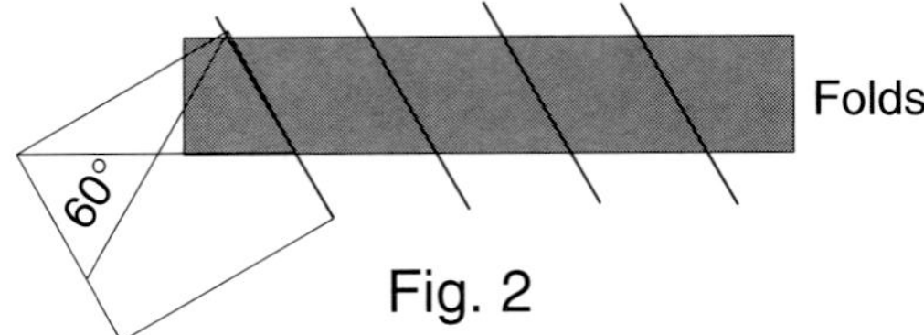

Fig. 2

PIECING
There are 14 rows, each containing (21) pieces. These rows are divided into two different piecing sequences. Make (7) strips of each sequence.

PIECING SEQUENCES

Row 1: A B A C A B A C A B A C A B A C A B A C A
Row 2: A C A B A C A B A C A B A C A B A C A B A
(Fig. 3, Fig. 4, Fig. 5 and Fig. 6.)

Sew pieces together as illustrated. The (<——>) refers to where the straight grain should be on the fabric pieces so the outside edges of the pieced strips will be on the straight-of-grain. Trim each seam and finger press it toward the diamond before adding the next piece to the row.

Sew together (7) sets of Row I and Row II. The seams do not butt each other, so matching each seam is more difficult. Sometimes a dab of glue stick in the seam allowance is helpful for holding two seams together. Sew the sets together. Trim the seams.

ASSEMBLY

1. First Border: Cut (1) 1" x 44" strip of light blue. Subcut to fit and stitch to the quilt using the straight-cut corner method. Press the seams toward the outside of the quilt.
2. Second Border: Cut (2) 1 7/8" x 44" strips of medium blue. Subcut to fit and stitch to the quilt using the straight-cut corner method. Press the seams toward the outside of the quilt.
3. Layer the quilt with thin batting and medium blue backing.
4. Quilt as desired.
5. Finish the quilt with navy blue binding.

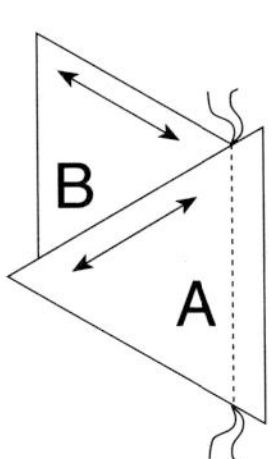

Fig. 3

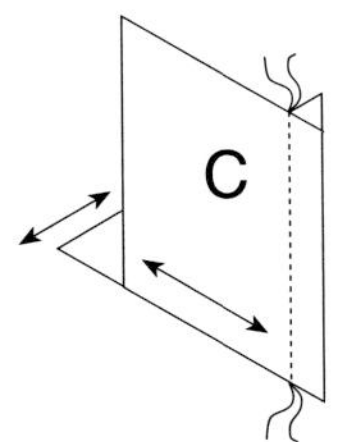

A on bottom

Fig. 4

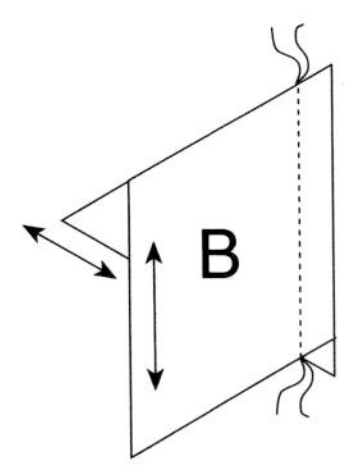

A on bottom

Fig. 5

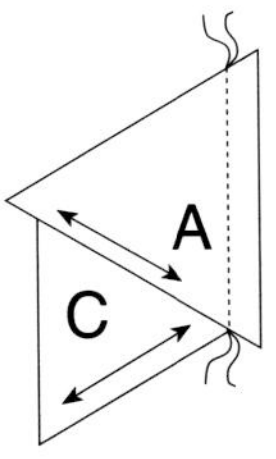

Fig. 6

SUNSHINE & SHADOW

quilt shown on page 34

14" Square

This pattern combines the Sunshine and Shadow with the Diamond in Square. The original 86" square quilt was made in Lancaster County, Pennsylvania, in 1930, and is now owned by Jay M. and Susen E. Leary. Lancaster County was the first permanent Amish settlement in America.

My tiny version consists of 3/8" finished squares and contains the same number of pieces as the original quilt.

Use 1/4" seam allowance; trim to 1/8" where needed to eliminate bulk.

FABRIC REQUIREMENTS

3/4 yard light red for inner border, first outer border and backing
1/4 yard dark teal for piecing and binding
1/4 yard light pink for piecing and setting triangles
1/8 yard purple for piecing and second outer border
1/8 yard medium green, dark pink, turquoise, bright red and lime green for piecing

CUTTING AND PIECING OF SUNSHINE AND SHADOW SECTIONS

1. Cut the following 7/8" wide strips:
Dark Teal: Cut (3) 44" strips and subcut (4) 12" strips, (1) 28" strip and (12) 7/8" squares.
Medium Green: Cut (2) 44" strips and subcut (4) 12" strips and (1) 28" strip.
Light Pink: Cut (2) 44" strips and subcut (3) 12" strips and (1) 28" strip.
Dark Pink: Cut (2) 44" strips and subcut (2) 12" strips and (1) 28" strip.
Purple: Cut (1) 44" strip and subcut (1) 12" strip and (1) 28" strip.
Turquoise: Cut (1) 28" strip.
Bright Red: Cut (1) 17" strip and subcut (2) 5" strips and (6) 7/8" squares.
Lime Green: Cut (1) 5" strip.

2. Make the following set-ups by sewing the 7/8" wide strips together lengthwise. Press seams toward dark teal strips. Some seams will have to be pressed again later.

(a) 12"
Medium Green
Dark Teal

Subcut (12) 7/8" segments.

(b) 12"
Light Pink
Medium Green
Dark Teal

Subcut (12) 7/8" segments.

(c) 12"
Dark Pink
Light Pink
Medium Green
Dark Teal

Subcut (12) 7/8" segments.

(d) 12"
Purple
Dark Pink
Light Pink
Medium Green
Dark Teal

Subcut (12) 7/8" segments.

(e) 28"
Turquoise
Purple
Dark Pink
Light Pink
Medium Green
Dark Teal

Subcut (28) 7/8" segments.

(f) 5"
Bright Red
Lime Green
Bright Red

Subcut (5) 7/8" segments.

3. Setting Triangles: Cut (2) 2 1/4" x 44" strips of light pink. Subcut (23) 2 1/4" squares and cut diagonally both ways to make (92) setting triangles.

4. Corner Triangles: Cut (4) 1 3/4" squares and cut diagonally in half to make (8) corner triangles.

5. Lay out strip segments, squares and triangles in correct sequence for the center diamond section according to the picture of the quilt. It is helpful to have a stabilizer underneath the units, such as a piece of flannel, felt or terry cloth.

Sew into 15 rows. Alternate the direction of the seams for each row. Some of the seams in a strip segment will need to be pressed again to go the same direction as the other seams in the row. Trim seams to 1/8". Stitch the rows together. Add the corners last. It may be necessary to straighten the block by steaming it and pulling it square. Pin it down and let it dry. Trim the setting and corner triangles evenly around the center diamond section, leaving a 1/4" seam allowance (Fig. 1).

Fig. 1

6. Make (4) Sunshine and Shadow corner triangle sections consisting of eight rows each. Follow the instructions for the center diamond section (Fig. 2).

Fig. 2

ASSEMBLY

1. Inner Border: Cut (1) 2 1/4" x 44" strip of light red. Sew to the edges of the center diamond section by mitering the corners (refer to section on Borders). Press seams toward the outside of the quilt.

2. Lay the Sunshine and Shadow corner triangle sections on the inner border edges. Measure the border width needed to accommodate the corner triangle sections. Trim the inner border to the size needed. Sew a corner triangle section to each side of the inner border. Be sure to place the center square of each triangle section right in the center of the border. Measure each border to mark the exact centers. Press the seams toward the inner borders.

3. First Outer Border: Cut (1) 1 5/8" x 44" strip of light red. Subcut to fit and stitch to the quilt using the straight-cut corner method. Press the seams to the outside of the quilt.

4. Second Outer Border: Cut (2) 2" x 44" strips of purple. Subcut to fit and stitch to the quilt using the straight-cut corner method. Press the seams toward the outside of the quilt.

5. Layer the quilt with thin batting and light red backing.

6. Quilt as desired.

7. Finish the quilt with dark teal binding.

LONE STAR

quilt shown on page 35

15 1/2" Square

The color scheme of an Amish Lone Star quilt dated January 11, 1927, inspired this miniature version. That original quilt was made in Ohio and is now owned by Diana Leone. My little quilt contains 288 diamonds like the antique quilt, but are only 3/8" in size. It is a challenge to sew and requires very precise cutting and piecing.

Use 1/4" seam allowance; trim to 1/8" where needed to eliminate bulk.

FABRIC REQUIREMENTS (Colors are identified by a letter to correspond with the color sequence of the Lone Star.)
Fabric A: 1/8 yard off-white for piecing and first border
Fabric B: 1/8 yard medium coral
Fabric C: 1/8 yard peach
Fabric D: 1/8 yard deep blue
Fabric E: 1/8 yard black for piecing and binding
1 yard dark coral for background, second border and backing

CUTTING
Fabric A: Cut (3) 7/8" x 44" strips and subcut into (8) 14" lengths.
Fabric B: Cut (1) 7/8" x 44" strip and subcut into (2) 14" lengths.
Fabric C: Cut (2) 7/8" x 44" strips and subcut into (6) 14" lengths.
Fabric D: Cut (4) 7/8" x 44" strips and subcut into (10) 14" lengths.
Fabric E: Cut (4) 7/8" x 44" strips and subcut into (10) 14" lengths.
Lightly press the strips.

PIECING OF DIAMONDS

1. Make (6) different sets of fabric strips as illustrated. Slowly sew the strips together lengthwise, being careful to keep the seams very straight. Chain-piece the first two strips of each set together at one time. Remove from the machine and clip the units apart. Press the seams toward the first strip of each set. Chain-piece the third strips to the second strips. Press the seams in the same direction. Repeat for the other strips (Fig. 1).

   Make sure the sets of fabric strips are all straight and not curved. If there is curvature, pin the set on the ironing board and steam to straighten it. Let it dry completely before moving it. Trim the seams to 1/8".
2. Turn each set so that the first strip is at the top. Align the 45° angle of a long ruler on a seamline of the set, and make a 45° angle cut. Now align the 7/8" line of the ruler on this cut angle and cut a 7/8" wide bias strip. Cut (8) 7/8" wide bias strips from each set. Check the 45° angle frequently and recut if necessary (Fig. 2).
3. Make (8) large diamonds from the bias strips. Take one strip from each set and lay the six strips in sequence as illustrated (Fig. 3). Before sewing two strips together, line up matching points of seam intersections on a positioning pin and pin next to it. Remove the positioning

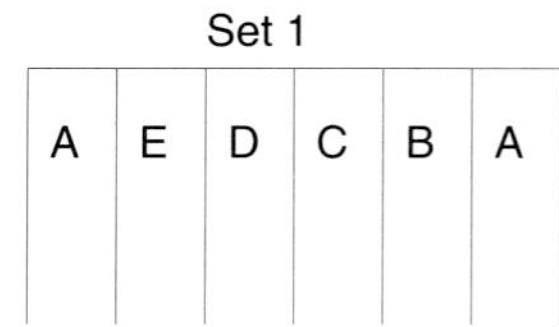

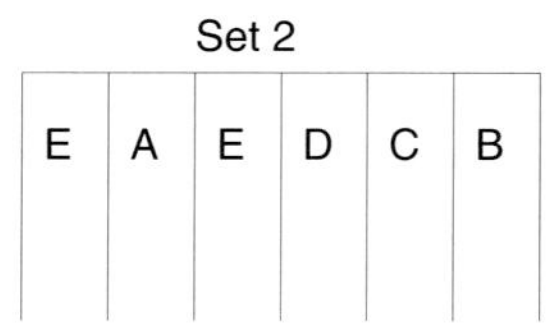

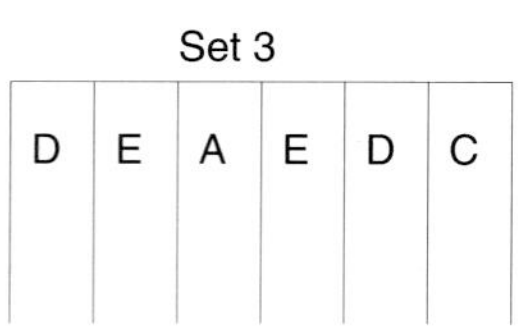

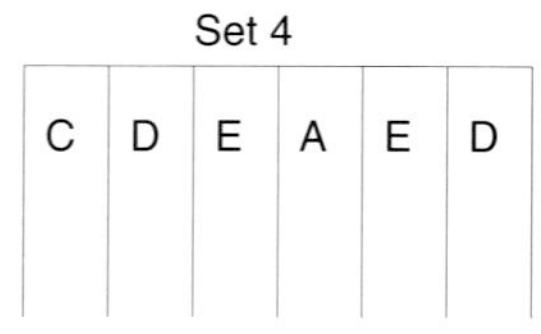

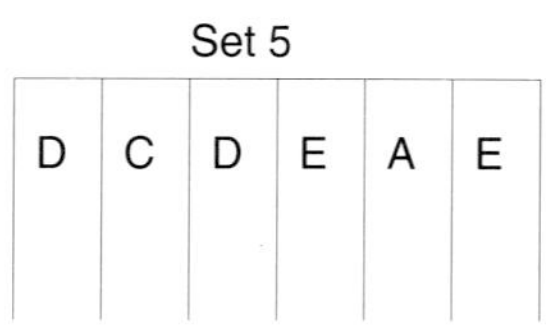

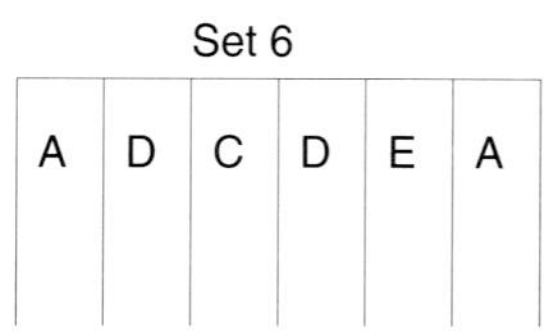

Fig. 1

pin.
HINT: Glue stick is very useful to match stubborn seam intersections. Use a dab in the seam allowance of the intersection. Press the seams in the direction of the arrow. Trim the seams to 1/8".

ASSEMBLY OF LONE STAR

1. Sew together two pieced diamonds (Fig. 4). Be careful to match seams. Stitch down from the part of the diamond which will be the center to 1/4" from the bottom edge and backstitch to secure the seam. It is helpful to first mark a pencil dot at the precise stopping point for these seams. Sew four sets. Sew to the dot and backstitch. Press seams to the right. Do not trim these seams.
2. Stitch these sets into two halves (Fig. 5). Press seams to the right. Do not trim these seams.
3. Sew two halves together. Start sewing 1/4" from one end and stop sewing 1/4" from the other. Be sure to backstitch at both ends. Carefully match the center where eight seams come together. A dab of glue stick may be helpful in the center seam allowance. Do not trim the seam. It may be pressed open or to one side.

ASSEMBLY OF QUILT

1. Setting Triangles: Cut (1) 7" square of background fabric and cut diagonally both ways to make (4) oversized triangles. These will be sewn between the four sets of diamonds with set-in seams. On the wrong side of the (4) triangles, mark a pencil dot exactly 1/4" from each side of the right angles at the top of the triangles (Fig. 6).

   Place a triangle wrong side up on top of the adjoining diamond unit and pin so that the dot meets the spot where the stitching ended between the two diamonds. Sew from the dot by backstitching to it and then sewing to the edge of the diamond. Sew the second diamond to the other side of the triangle by pivoting the triangle to meet the other diamond. Pin and sew from the intersection by backstitching to it and then sewing to the edge of the diamond. The triangles will extend beyond the diamonds. Press the seams toward the background fabric.
2. Corner Squares: Cut (4) 4" squares of background fabric. These squares are oversized. Mark a pencil dot exactly 1/4" in from the right angles in one corner of each square. Sew these squares into the corners of the Lone Star with set-in seams. Press the seams toward the background fabric (Fig. 7).
3. Trim the quilt top evenly, leaving a 1/4" seam allowance from the end points of the Lone Star.
4. First Border: Cut (2) 1 1/4" x 44" strips of off-white. Subcut to fit and stitch to the quilt using the straight-cut corner method. Press the seams toward the outside of the quilt.
5. Second Border: Cut (2) 2 1/4" x 44" strips of dark coral. Subcut to fit and stitch to the quilt using the straight-cut corner method. Press the seams toward the outside of the quilt.
6. Layer the quilt with thin batting and dark coral backing.
7. Quilt as desired.
8. Finish the quilt with black binding.

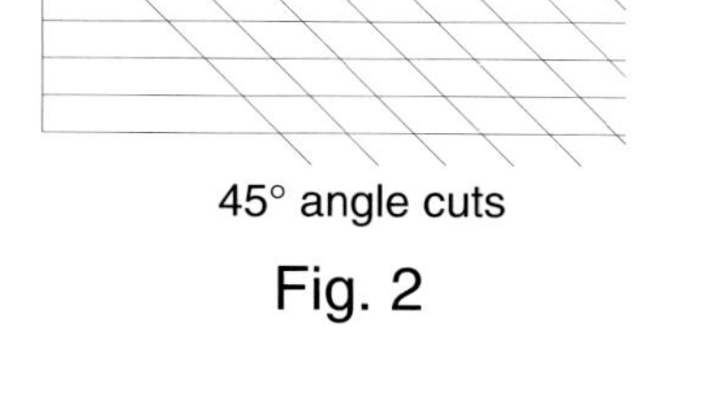

Fig. 2

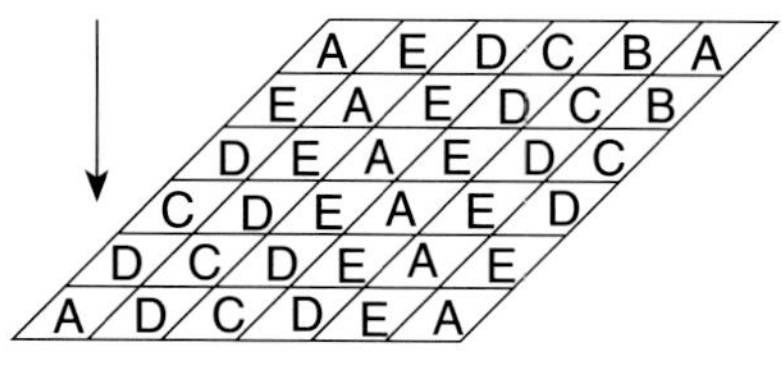

Fig. 3

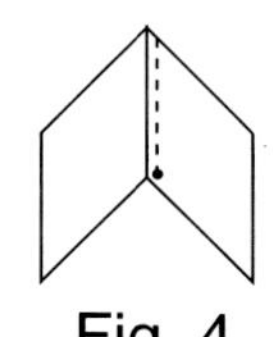
Fig. 4

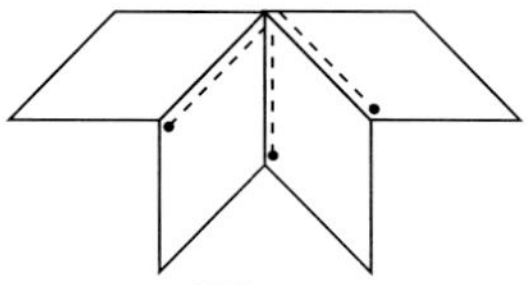

Fig. 5

Fig. 7

Fig. 6

BIBLIOGRAPHY

Bishop, Robert, and Elizabeth Safanda, *A Gallery Of Amish Quilts, Design Diversity from a Plain People*, E. P. Dutton, New York, 1976.

Good, Merle and Phyllis Good, *20 Most Asked Questions About the Amish and Mennonites*, Good Books, Lancaster, PA, 1979.

Hopkins, Mary Ellen, *Connecting Up*, ME Publications, Santa Monica, CA, 1990.

Pellman, Rachel T., and Joanne Ranck, *Quilts Among the Plain People*, Good Books, Lancaster, PA, 1981.

Pellman, Rachel and Kenneth Pellman, *A Treasury of Amish Quilts*, Good Books, Intercourse, PA, 1990.

______, *The World of Amish Quilts*, Good Books, Intercourse, PA, 1984.

ALSO BY CHITRA PUBLICATIONS

Magazines
Miniature Quilts • *Quilting Today* • *Traditional Quiltworks*
For subscription information, write to Chitra Publications, 2 Public Avenue, Montrose, PA 18801, or call 1-800-628-8244 (M-F, 8-4:30 EST)

Books
- *The Best of Miniature Quilts, Volume 1* compiled by Patti Lilik Bachelder
- *Designing New Traditions in Quilts* by Sharyn Squier Craig
- *Drafting Plus: 5 Simple Steps to Pattern Drafting and More!* by Sharyn Squier Craig
- *Quilting Design Treasury* by Anne Szalavary
- *Small Folk Quilters* by Ingrid Rogler
- *A Stitcher's Christmas Album* by Patti Lilik Bachelder
- *Theorem Appliqué, Book I: Abundant Harvest* (Book I of IV) by Patricia B. Campbell and Mimi Ayars, Ph.D.
- *Tiny Traditions* by Sylvia Trygg Voudrie